Made in His Image

Made in His Image

PABLO LUCERO

His Place Press
Albuquerque, New Mexico

©2019 by Pablo Lucero

HIS PLACE PRESS
5505 Central NW
Albuquerque, New Mexico 87105

Library of Congress Control Number: 2019930024
ISBN: 978-1-7335637-0-3

Cover tatoo design: Pablo Lucero
Cover photographs: (man) jcfotographo; (bird) Ackley Road Photos/Adobe Stock
Digital composite: J.M. Ritz
Editing & book design by J.M. Ritz

Printed in the United States

CHAPTER 1

Drought

Nobody expected me to live when I was born. My mom gave birth to triplets at home, and two of the triplets were born dead. The *curandera* (healer) who delivered us called me a blue baby and said I wouldn't survive, either. So my parents gave me a throw-away name, Pablo, because they didn't think I was going to last.

While my mom was recuperating, my dad put cotton in his shoebox and then set me in a little side area of the wood stove to keep me warm. Then he mixed water with oatmeal and fed me the milk. My two older brothers, Florencio and Richard, helped watch over me. Everyone expected me to die, but to everyone's surprise, I lived.

Over the next few years, my mother gave birth to two more sons.

Our family lived on a small farm in the mountains east of Albuquerque, near Escabosa. My parents were bean farmers, and we lived off the land. Our closest neighbor was a mile away. My dad had the best pair of horses in the mountains. It would take him three days to ride into Albuquerque, and three days to ride back.

It was the mid 1940s, and our farm wasn't getting any rain. Because of the dry conditions, my dad couldn't get the bean plants to grow. By then, my parents had five boys to feed, and we were going hungry, so when I was four, my dad sold the farm. We loaded up our two horses, and my parents moved us to Los Ranchos, north of Albuquerque.

My dad got a job in Los Ranchos working for the Yoromoro brothers in the strawberry and potato fields. We rented a small house surrounded by the fields where my dad worked. Once again there was plenty of food to eat and life was good for us. After a year or so my mom gave birth to a sixth child, this time a girl.

My dad was strict and kept us all close. If he said that you should be there for breakfast or lunch, then you would be there. There was never any profanity in our house. Me and my brothers never got into fights. My dad kept us together as a tight unit.

One night, my dad was walking home from work, carrying a sack of potatoes on his back for our dinner. In those days there were few, if any, street lights, and he was walking along the road in the dark.

Just before he turned off onto the road to our house, a semi-truck came up from behind him. The driver must not have seen my dad because the truck hit him. My dad was killed on the spot.

CHAPTER 2

The Sucker

We buried my dad in a coffin made of tomato crates. We had a wake for him that lasted three days, and then the field workers dug his grave and buried him. In the days after my dad passed away, the field workers threw us sacks of potatoes over the barbed wire fence so we would have something to eat.

My mom couldn't afford our house without my dad's income, so with the little money my parents had saved, she moved all seven of us into two small rooms behind the general store in Alameda.

I remember one night after we had moved behind the store, somebody gave me a nickel. I was about seven at the time, and I used to wear little overalls. We called them *pecheras*. I put the nickel in the pocket of my pecheras where I could keep it safe. I couldn't wait for the store to open the next day, so I could get me a candy.

In the morning, I got up extra early while everyone was still sleeping because I wasn't going to share the candy with my brothers. I put on my pecheras and went to the store.

When I walked inside, a man was already there at the counter, and I got in line behind him, waiting to buy a sucker. The store owner came from the back, carrying a box of groceries for the man, and set the box on the glass countertop. Then, he and this man got into a conversation.

Finally, they stopped talking, and the man was ready to pay for his groceries. The only problem was that the man couldn't find his money. He looked on the floor and then went through his pockets again, but he still couldn't find his money.

The owner spotted me standing there in line, and he must have thought I took the money because he walked around the counter, grabbed me by the pecheras, and tossed me out the door like a puppet. Then he walked outside and kicked my butt. I was just a kid, and I was so scared I peed my pants and started crying.

A few minutes later, the customer came out and told the owner he had found his money underneath his grocery box on the counter. The owner went back inside and left me there crying.

My brother Richard must have heard all the noise because he came out and asked me what had happened. I told him the whole story. Later, the store owner came back out and brought me a sucker. He said he was sorry. But by then it was too late.

That night, my brothers Flo and Richard knocked a hole through the wall of our bedroom and broke into the store. They got me a sucker and a lot of other stuff.

The next day, when the store owner saw the hole in the wall, he figured out what had happened. He called my mom into the store, and he kicked us all out.

CHAPTER 3

Martineztown

My dad had an insurance policy through his work, but my mom didn't know how to read or write, so she couldn't manage it. So when my dad died, my uncles took control of the insurance money.

After we got kicked out of the store, my uncles bought us a two-room shack in Martineztown in Albuquerque with some of the insurance money. After that, they wiped their hands of my mom and our family, and they never came back. They cut us loose.

While we were living in Los Ranchos, my mom had started going out with a man who was a rancher. She was a pretty woman, and the rancher had fallen in love with her. The rancher was the kindest man we had ever met. He didn't drink. He didn't cuss. He had a ranch with horses and cows, and, most importantly, he liked all of us. The whole family. If my mom had married him, our family would have had a very different life than the one we had.

The rancher helped us to move into our new house in Albuquerque. The house we moved into was an adobe house with just two rooms, the bedroom and the kitchen, and there was no partition between the rooms. It had a wood stove, and they brought in a table with four chairs. My mom got a bed for herself and my sister and a bunkbed for the rest of us.

I remember not long after we moved in, my mom was making a big pot of beans at the stove. The rancher was sitting at the kitchen table, and a man who lived next door came into the house.

The rancher noticed that my mom was google-eyeing this man. Then he watched the neighbor walk up behind my mom and say something to her. The rancher must not have liked what he heard because he walked over and punched the man. Then he beat him up.

My mom threw the rancher out. And she stayed with the neighbor. This guy wasn't a violent man, but he was a wino, a drunk. We used to take care of him.

There were too many of us to sleep in the bunkbed my mom got us, so it was first come, first served. Whoever showed up last, didn't get a bed and slept on the floor. We had an outhouse and a water pump outside. We used to take turns filling the tub. We all took a bath in the same water, starting from the oldest to the youngest.

Every day, my mom made fresh tortillas out of lard and flour. Then she made beans or soup, using whatever she could. Each week, I walked with her down to Barelas where the government passed out blocks of cheese, pork, powdered milk, and powdered eggs. My job was to put the food in a little red wagon and pull it home. The food never lasted us the whole week.

My oldest brother, Flo, was fourteen when we moved to Martineztown. I remember going to the fiestas in Martinez-town with my brothers and my sister. We sat there in the tent, watching the dancers while Florencio was at home getting ready to go out. When he was ready to leave, he walked into the tent. All he had to do was glance at us with his eyes, and we all stood up and went home. We had respect. Flo never had any hassle from any of us.

CHAPTER 4

A Little Cross

None of us had ever been to school while we lived in Alameda, but when we moved to Martineztown, my mom enrolled me at Longfellow Elementary.

They put me in the third grade because of my age, but I didn't know how to read or write like the other kids, and I didn't speak English. My parents and everyone else around me spoke Spanish. We spoke the kind of Spanish that goes way back to the first settlers of New Mexico.

But at that time, all of the lessons in school were in English, and I only understood Spanish. By the time I got into the sixth grade, I understood English, but I hadn't learned how to read or write. My teacher used to put me in the hall, and I would sit out there all day. No paper, *ni nada* (no nothing). Just me in a chair.

My mom used to patch my pants with Masa Harina flour bags. After she used the flour to make tortillas, she cut up the flour sacks and patched our clothes. And I didn't want to go to school with Gold Medal flour pants. I was ashamed of those patched clothes.

In those days, everybody would hang their laundry outside on the clothesline to dry. So I started dressing myself from the clotheslines. I would walk through the barrio, and if I saw a pair of pants that I liked, even if they fit me real big, I would take them. I would use a popsicle stick to keep them secure. I invented the large pants that kids love nowadays. I would throw a shirt over them, and just like that I had clean clothes.

At one point, my mom started to receive a check each month from the government. She would take the check to a little store in Martineztown where they sold food and other things. I used to go with her and she'd pick out eggs, canned beans, Spam, and a loaf of bread.

When it was time to pay, I remember watching her take the pen and carefully draw a little cross on the back of the check for her signature. She didn't know how to write her name. She also didn't know how to count money. If you had a twenty-dollar bill here and five ones there, she would take the five ones, thinking it was more money.

When I got older, I noticed that other people with checks were getting more food than her. She would come out of the store with just two little bags, no change, no nothing. So I started asking around. We showed the check to our neighbors, and they told us we should be getting more food. So we figured out that the store was ripping us off.

My friends and I used to hang around Martineztown by Santa Barbara, up there on the hill. One of the guys had a little tent in the back of his house, and we started hanging out back there with a five-gallon bucket of glue. We sniffed glue all day to get loaded.

One day we were sitting in the tent, sniffing glue, and we were talking about our families. I told my friends, "You know, I think my mom's being ripped off by this store owner."

One of my friends agreed, "I think that store really rips people off. There's a few stores around here that are ridiculous."

We decided to go hit that store. We broke in at night, and we took everything we could—all the food we could carry. We never got caught.

CHAPTER 5

Holding Heavy

In my days, growing up in the barrio, we had control of
our neighborhoods. If you lived in Barelas or San Jose, you
couldn't just come over to Martineztown because you felt
like it. You had to ask permission.

I remember, one day, a guy from another barrio came into
our neighborhood, and me and my brothers jumped him
like ants and beat him up. I grabbed a piece of fence with
nails in it, and I hit the guy with it while he was crawling
on the ground.

We all knew that if you went into someone else's neighborhood, you had to ask permission. That's how we kept
control. If somebody who wasn't from our barrio was walking down our street, it was because he had permission. I had

permission to go to all of the barrios because I used to hang out with the little brothers of the gang members.

The gangs ran the barrios, and they respected each other. Nobody messed with the women. Your sister could walk the streets at night, and she didn't need protection. Because she had the protection of the whole barrio. They all knew her. All the guys would hang out on the corner, all dressed up, but she could go anywhere, and there would be no profanity, no whistling, no "Hey! Baby." Because if they did, there would be problems.

Even the elderly people were respected. An old man would send you to the store for a pack of cigarettes. And you'd better go. And don't cheat him.

My brothers and I had control of our neighborhood, but it was a different story inside our house. At home, when my mom had a wino stay over, I had to stay outside. Even as a little kid, they put me outside to sleep when a wino came over. It didn't matter if it was summer or winter.

Sometimes, one of the winos would come over drunk and throw the house and get violent with my mom. When I was little, I would stay outside and cry and try to find a place to hide in the yard. When I got older, I'd leave and go find an ally to sleep in.

When I was still in school, my brother Flo moved out of the house. He had started dealing drugs to bring money in. By the time I was a teenager, Flo had about ten dealers working with him. Flo would give a guy five caps to sell. The guy could keep two, and then bring Flo three. That's how he made his money.

Flo also had a beautiful girlfriend. They called her "Sexy." Sexy was Flo's mule. She would go to Juarez to bring heroin in. I remember going with Flo to pick her up at the bus station when she came back from Juarez.

After Sexy brought the heroin back, Flo cut it in the house with brown sugar. Then he tested it. A man named Flaco was the tester. Every time Flaco tested, he'd fall off the stool, until it was cut right. Once it was cut right, and he felt normal, then they'd pack it and sell it.

Florencio was very particular about his appearance. He was always dressed to kill, and he always wore hats. They called them *panos*.

In the crazy life, if you're holding heavy, you need workers. Flo had the whole neighborhood, all the *Vatos Locos* (Crazy Guys), coming early in the morning. Two vatos would be inside shining his shoes, and two would be outside cleaning his Cadillac.

My brother Richard started dealing, too.

CHAPTER 6

Setup

In those days, the city assigned a couple of detectives to each barrio. My barrio was covered by two detectives, Torres and Proffer. Those people would jump you from on top of the tree or whatever to take you in.

One day, I was sitting on our porch waiting for a friend, and I heard somebody running, and somebody else behind him yelling, "Halt! Halt! Police!"

I walked out into the alley, and I saw my brother, Richard, running towards me, followed by the *jura*. That's what we called the police.

"Richard, get over here!" I called out.

Richard ran over to me, and I said, "Take off your shirt."

I put on his shirt, and then I started running up the ally. The policeman thought I was Richard because I was wearing his shirt, so he started chasing me. I took him around Lomas, Edith, around the filling station back to Arnold. I got back to the alley and Richard and I switched shirts again, and then Richard took off. Two or three times we ran around until finally, the policeman fell to his knees, completely out of breath.

There was a guy named Lalo, and he used to push for Flo, in the barrio. One time, Torres and Proffer caught him with heroin in his pocket. But instead of arresting him, they just put the heroin back in his pocket and let him go. They had a strategy. They were setting him up to look like a rat, but he wasn't. I saw a lot of guys get wasted that way.

Once a guy in our barrio named Manuel got set up by the jura to look like a rat. Manuel was a big guy, and he was covered with tatoos. He was a heavy pusher from Barelas, and when he moved to Martineztown, the jura set him up.

One day they called Manuel in, and they threatened to sentence his mother to prison for harboring a trafficker. To save his mother, Manuel made a deal with them. He had a lot of brothers, and he was a guy that you didn't mess with, but he had made a deal with the police to save his mother, and so he got pegged as a rat.

One day, I was sitting in a car with the window rolled down with a friend of mine. I was telling him about someone who had ratted out my little brother Rosie in school. "*Estos ratas* (those rats), they'll rat anybody out!" I told him.

Just as I said that, Manuel was passing by. He must have heard me because he walked over to the car window where I was sitting. Then he pulled out his gun and put it to my head.

"What did you say about *ratas*?" he said.

"I didn't say nothing," I said.

"Good," he said.

All the guys in the barrio used to get gas at a filling station down the street. We had a friend who worked there, a wino, named Benny. Benny ran the filling station. Manuel used to walk over to the filling station and spend time with Benny.

One day, Benny worked out a plan with three guys to pull an armed robbery on the filling station. That way, Benny could split the money with them. So one afternoon, the three guys walked into the filling station and told Benny to empty the cash register.

While they were taking the money, Manuel walked in. Benny already knew about the robbery, but Manuel didn't know. So when Manuel walked in and saw the guys holding up his friend Benny, he drew a knife out of his boot.

The guys doing the robbery had the idea that Manuel was a rat, so one of the guys pointed his shotgun at Manuel and blew his chest off. Manuel went through the window. That's how he died.

So the setup of a policeman could be life or death.

CHAPTER 7

Detention

I stopped going to school when I was in the sixth grade. Instead of going to class, I hid out in a ditch during the day, so the truant officers wouldn't find me. I was also sniffing glue and gasoline to get high. I would unscrew the gasoline caps on cars and sniff the gas until POP! I'd be an electrician, seeing hundreds and thousands of sparks in front of me. By the time I was done, the car was drained of all its gas.

One day, a truant officer found me sniffing gas and threw me in the detention home on Broadway. I was scared the first time I went to the detention home, but later on, detention became a routine. It became like a home. I got to sleep. I got to take a shower. I got to eat. The only thing that was different was that I couldn't leave.

The superintendent, a woman named Miss Farrell, ran the home. When Miss Farrell walked through the hallways, she would take off her high heels, so she wouldn't make noise. That way she could catch the guys who were smoking or doing what they weren't supposed to.

We had one radio in the home, and one day, when Miss Farrell went to turn it on, it was broken. So she launched an investigation. She called me in, sat me down in a chair, and gave me a sucker. She waited a few seconds until I put the sucker in my mouth, and then she asked me who had touched the radio.

I've never been somebody who would tell anybody anything, so I wouldn't talk. I just sat there enjoying my candy. Miss Farrell asked me second time, and when I didn't answer, she slapped me so hard the sucker flew out of my mouth and skidded across the floor. But I still didn't talk. The way I looked at it, what are you going to change?

When I finished my time in detention, my mother would come and pick me up. At first, she tried putting me back into school, but I would just leave again, and then I'd be back in detention.

After I had been in detention several times, my mom drove me out to a farm in Alameda to stay with a woman I called *Tia*, Auntie, even though she wasn't really my aunt. She was a little old lady, tiny and bent down. She spoke Spanish like my parents. Her husband was a WWII veteran, and they had a house and a farm.

Tia took care of a lot of kids like me. At night, I used to sleep on the floor with about five other kids, and we would get up in the morning and feed the pigs and chickens and chop wood. Tia was like a mother to me. If any of the other kids tried to pick on me, she yelled at them.

One time, I was out riding my bike and the police started chasing me. I don't remember what I did. But I remember, I was trying to get away from them, and I crossed the road in front of a semi. The driver swerved to keep from hitting me, and he flipped his truck. I went and hid at Tia's.

The driver told the police what had happened, and the police walked around the neighborhood looking for me. When they came to Tia's door, she said to me, "Stay here." She talked to the police, but she didn't say anything about me. The police looked everywhere, but they never found me.

One day, I was walking to Albuquerque to see my mom. On the way, I got picked up by a truant officer, and they threw me back in detention.

Each time I got put in detention, I had to go to court. This time, when I was walking down the hallway on my way to the courtroom, I noticed a patrol uniform hanging on a hook. In those days, they used patrol boys to patrol the schools and help keep order. The patrol boys all wore a red coat, a hat, and a strap with a white badge on it.

When I saw the uniform, I got an idea. If I were a patrol boy, the judge might have leniency on me. He would think, "Oh, this is a patrol boy!" and then let me go.

So before I walked into the courtroom, I stopped in the hall and put on the hat, the red coat, and the white badge. Then I walked into the court room dressed like a patrol boy. As soon as the police saw me, they stripped me of the patrol uniform and threw me in jail.

After I got out of jail, I hung out on the streets and took care of myself. I slept in bus stops and under bridges.

For food, I'd catch about three or four pigeons. In those days people put metal milk baskets in front of their doors for milkmen to leave milk. I found one of those baskets, turned it upside down, propped it up with a pole, and put some crackers inside. I tied a string around the pole, then I went and hid.

When the pigeon went under the carton to get the crackers, I pulled the string. SNAP! Then I plucked and cleaned him. I looked for butter and salt in the trash behind restaurants, and when I found some, I cooked the pigeons in butter.

I used to go under the bridges at night and light a little fire. The guys would come and sit around the fire, and we'd smoke and talk, and I would share my pigeons. Some guys thought it was chicken.

I was familiar with pigeons because my brother Flo raised them. He kept giant pigeons in cages. He called them "the tanks," and he used them to deliver drugs.

Here and there, I would stay over at my mom's place. I didn't stay with her often because she didn't have room, and I never wanted to take anything from my mom. But one night, I was staying with my mom. After sleeping in allies and bus stops, sleeping on a couch was luxury, and that night, I quickly fell into a deep sleep.

But my rest didn't last long. In the early morning, right before it was light, I woke up to somebody kicking in the door.

CHAPTER 8

Arrested

It was 1960 and the police were conducting *los arrastres*. They were doing a sweep of the barrios and catching everybody who was selling drugs.

After the jura kicked in our door, they yanked me out of bed, handcuffed me to a chair, and searched the house. They kept calling me Richard, but I wasn't going to volunteer that I wasn't Richard. Whatever they called me, they called me.

The police ransacked the house looking for drugs. One of them called out, "Here it is! I've got it!"

My mom had a lot of powders for *remedios* (medicines) and the police bagged them all up. They thought they had found heroin.

As they were taking me out the door, I called to my little brother Rosie to tell Richard *que poner a truchas*—to look out because the police were looking for him. The police were Anglos, so they didn't speak Spanish. At that time, Richard was renting a house in Alameda with his girlfriend. The police had come to my mom's house looking for Richard, but they got me instead.

When they took me to jail, they threw me in jail with a lot of gang members from the barrios. The police were taking the vatos downstairs and putting us in a lineup. At least, that's what we thought.

When I had left my house, I didn't have a shirt on, so I grabbed a shirt that belonged to my brother Flo. Flo was in prison at that time, and he was keeping his clothes at my mom's house.

A guy named Masca was with me in the cell, and after looking at me, he said, "Hey, why don't you lend me that shirt?"

He thought that if he had a nice shirt on, they wouldn't recognize him in the lineup. So I loaned Masca Flo's shirt, and he put it on. Then the police took him. When they brought Masca back, he was all beat up, and Flo's shirt was torn to pieces.

"They're not putting anybody on the line," Masca told us. "They're beating us all up."

I didn't know how I was going to tell Florencio that his shirt was gone. I was more afraid of Florencio than I was of the jura.

Then the police took me downstairs. I was standing in front of a desk without a shirt and one of them asked me, "Where'd you put the stuff?"

"What stuff?"

"Who do you hang around with, and who's your connection?"

"I don't know what you're talking about."

BOOM! One of the jura hit me across the face, grabbed me by the handcuffs, and threw me over the desk. Then he beat me up and gave me a black eye.

I couldn't tell them names even if I had wanted to. We didn't know names on purpose. Because if someone beats you up looking for names, how are you going to tell what you don't know?

When they found out I wasn't Richard, they tried to get me for impersonating Richard.

"Why were you pretending to be your brother?" they asked me.

"You never asked my name," I told them. "You were the ones who blew it."

After that, they let me out. They put all of my mom's medicines in a bag, handed them to me, and kicked me out of jail.

Later, I told Flo about his shirt. He was pissed when he found out about it, but he didn't do nothing to me. What could he do? He was locked up.

CHAPTER 9

Friday Night Fights

After I got kicked out of jail, I went right back to living in the street. In those days, if you didn't have a job and you were loitering around, the police would throw you in jail for vagrancy. For not having a job. For not having an address. When the police approached me, I never gave them an address, so they just locked me up.

They locked me up, let me out, locked me up again.

The county jail was on First Street. The jail had steel slash windows that opened with a crank. I used to open the window and then lower a string in the alley and send a *kite* (message) to my brother Richard. Then Richard would bring something for me, maybe marijuana if I were lucky. He tied it to the string, and I would pull it up.

I always shared it with the other inmates, and we would all get loaded. Then I would start the Friday night fights.

The jail had a big pen where they had tables. That's where we used to take our trays and eat, in *el comedor*. On Friday night, the police brought in the winos and held them in the comedor. The jail was packed with winos.

I had a special hate for winos. I hated winos with a passion. Maybe it was because of the way the winos got violent with my mom when I was little.

So on Friday nights, they brought the winos in, and I told the guys, "OK, you want to bet on the fights?"

"What fights?" they asked.

"Just watch. I'm about to start them."

I went to the bathroom and got a cup of water from the toilet. Then, I threw the water over the side wall into the comedor and splashed a guy in the back who was standing up.

He thought the guy behind him was peeing on him, so he turned around and BOOM! The Friday night fights were on. All the winos started slugging each other, and then the police and the guards got involved, trying to separate them. That was our Friday night entertainment.

Sometimes my brother Richard and I were in jail at the same time. One time, Richard and I were eating in the comedor with another guy named Leroy from Socorro. He had been a paratrooper. Two Anglo guys from Alabama were sitting at the other end of the table, and one of them, called Red Colorado, was looking at a *Playboy* magazine. I told Leroy, "What's that guy doing? Look, he's looking at a *Playboy*."

Leroy looked over at the magazine and said, "Do you think if I asked him for it, he'd lend it to me?"

"No, I don't think so, man," I said. "*Pero*, if you want to, you can go and tear a page out."

So Leroy got up and went and tore a page out.

BOOM! another fight started. They were fighting so hard, and they got so tired that Richard and I went over and ate their lunch. We got dessert *y todo*.

When I wasn't in jail, I used to hang out with a guy named Ray. Ray and I used to sleep in the allies and get into trouble together.

Once, Ray got us jobs cleaning offices. We cleaned the offices at night, and every time we went to the office, Ray would ransack the desks for petty cash.

One night, we were about done, and I was outside sweeping. I remember I looked up, and two jura were standing there, dressed in suits. They brought Ray out, and they put us both up against the wall and searched us. They didn't find any money on me, but they found money on Ray and arrested him. Somebody must have reported us.

As they were taking Ray in, I called out, "Hey, I'm with him. I also took some money."

I didn't want them to take Ray and leave me behind. I didn't want them to separate us. So the police took me in, too. That's how I wound up doing time in Springer.

Springer was the state correctional institute. They called it "La Corre."

CHAPTER 10

La Corre

The hardest part of Springer was surviving. There were fights all the time. The barrios didn't get along. Santa Fe and Albuquerque didn't get along.

In Springer, you had to join a gang for protection. I was part of the Albuquerque gang.

I didn't go to Springer alone. Ray was with me. My brother Richard and another friend of mine, Mogli, were already there doing time.

When I first got into Springer, I had to learn fast how things worked. The guards throw everyone in a dorm, and if more guys from Santa Fe are in there, then you've got to watch your *p*'s and *q*'s, or they'll jump you. If there's more of them, then they control the dorm. You don't talk to them. You don't cross that line. They start acting smart. They might slap you around, beat you up, give you a black eye, and there's nothing you can do about it because you're outnumbered.

When Ray and I first got to Springer, the Albuquerque guys were outnumbered, but we just waited. At Springer the guys were in and out. The Santa Fe guys might have control for a while, but then some of them would get moved out, and Albuquerque guys would get moved in. Then there were more of us from Albuquerque, and it was time for us to control. That's when we took our revenge.

I knew some twins from Barelas, and they both had blue eyes. One of the twins got sent to Springer, and he and I became good friends. One night, I overheard some guys from Santa Fe saying they were going to jump him. So the next day, I gave my friend some skin. I warned him, "They're going to jump you tonight, the guys from Santa Fe."

That night, I kept a watch on him, and when the guys from Santa Fe came over to him, I stood up with him. When I stood up, then Ray stood up. Then Mogli stood up. Then the other guys stood up, and there was no problem. The guys from Santa Fe backed off.

During the day, we worked. My brother Richard worked in *la boila*, the boiler room, but I worked unloading the coal from the trains. Shoveling the coal caused a lot of dust, and I was blacker than black by the end of the day. The prison also used to hire us out to the farmers at Eagle Nest.

One evening, after we got back from working in the fields, I was throwing the ball out in the yard with some of my homies. A guy who was a boxer came running by, and as he passed us, Mogli flipped him off and said something to him.

The boxer didn't see Mogli flip him off, but he heard what he said, so he stopped and turned around and looked at me.

I just happened to have my eyes on him because I was watching to see what would happen. So he thought it was me who had said something to him. But he didn't do anything. He just went on his way.

On Sunday mornings, the guards would let us sleep in, and then in the afternoon they would take us down the hill into town and let us go to the movies.

That Sunday morning, I was lying in bed, sleeping, and an officer from the dorm came in. He walked over to my bed and threw a big ol' pair of boxing gloves down next to me. The gloves were almost as big as me.

"They want you outside," he said.

I got out of bed and carried the boxing gloves outside. The first thing I saw was a guy with gloves on, shadow boxing with a tree. It was the same guy who Mogli had flipped off in the yard.

My first thought was this guy is going to take me out, because I didn't know how to box. I had never even put on a pair of gloves.

Then I looked at the crowd of guys standing around watching, waiting for the fight, and I knew I didn't have a choice.

The guards put the gloves on me, and I stepped forward. Guys crowded in on all sides, forming a ring. Sure enough, this guy popped me a couple of times, and I went down. I got up, and he knocked me down again.

Now, I couldn't read or write, but I knew that if someone beat me up in front of everyone, and I did nothing, then it was all over for me.

So I took off my gloves and threw them aside. Then I did it my way. I did the street fight. In street fighting there are no rules. You do whatever it takes. This guy was a boxer, and he still had his gloves on, and I just went at him.

First, I kicked him in the groin, and when he bent down, I jumped him, popping him all over the place. The guards jumped in and grabbed me, pulling me off him. Then, they threw me into the hole.

CHAPTER 11

The Hole

When you go to the hole, you go by yourself, and you stay there. You don't get out for any reason. You don't go to the yard. You don't go to the movies. You don't get visits. I never had a visit anyway. You don't get nothing. You're just in your cell. They seclude you and try and mess with your mind.

They used to give me little green peas with my meals. I let them dry out, and I played marbles with them all day to keep myself occupied. I kept my mind busy with exercise and thinking of things other than doing time. Time is time. It's just when you're in the hole, the time goes a lot slower than working in the field.

They also take away your good time when you're in the hole. If you work in the fields, they take time off your sentence.

But if you get thrown in the hole, you lose all the good time you've earned.

But I didn't care. So what? I had been in the hole all my life. Sleeping in an ally, living under a bridge, trapped in a cell. It's all the same thing. When I got out of the hole, I went back to business as usual.

I didn't communicate with the guards, but I remember one guard named Juan. He was a big man, and he made us buff the dorm floors by hand with a cloth. Everybody would get underneath the beds in lines and buff the floor in silence. If you talked, Juan would come up and kick you in the stomach. If you got up, you would get the right hand.

Some days, Juan sat in his rocking chair, and then he would line us up in front of him. He would look at a guy and say, "Come here!"

Juan had a little glove on, and when the guy would walk over and stand in front of him, Juan would hit him in the chest, POP! and swing him to the side. It wasn't because we had broken any rules. Some of the guards were just mean. They weren't our kind of people.

Ray's brother Poncho was in Springer with us. One day, Juan called Poncho out of the lineup and told him to stand in front of him. Poncho did what Juan said, and I remember Juan hit him so hard that he broke Poncho's chest. But who was Poncho going to tell? The judge? The police? Who?

While doing time at Springer, sometimes I helped the priest. I was an altar boy. Before the service, the priest would send me to the *cuartito*, a little room in the back of the chapel, to bring him a bottle of bourbon.

This wasn't the fruit of the vine they talk about. It ain't the juice he gave to the people in the little cups. This was a pure bourbon.

I used to go in there and get the bourbon for the priest. But while I was in the cuartito, I would have a little cup myself. By the time I got it to him, I was all messed up, too.

I was an altar boy, but I was never religious. When I was growing up, my family didn't go to church. We just went to funerals.

In those days, at a funeral, people hired ladies we called *lloronas*, criers. The lloronas sat behind a curtain in the back, sobbing, like they knew the guy. If the family wanted it louder, they just showed the lloronas another ten-dollar bill. Sobs increase. That's the way it worked in those days.

Martineztown had a little church and people used to go and light the candles in front of the alter. It was twenty-five cents a candle and people would drop twenty-five cents down a hole.

Sometimes I went in there when it was empty. I took one of the long sticks used to light the candles, and I put a piece of gum on the end of the stick and picked up all the coins

I could. Then, with my pockets full of change, I lit all of the candles and went inside the church and sat down to rest.

Sometimes I even prayed. Like, when I was getting ready to steal something, I would pray, "Eeee, Lord, help me not get caught today."

Even though I wasn't religious, I had some sense that there was something else other than myself. We're all like that.

CHAPTER 12

Jumping Trains

I did my time at Springer, and when I got out, I went straight back to the streets. I must have been about fifteen or sixteen years old. I didn't find work. I was illiterate. I didn't know nothing about nothing. Except I knew how to steal.

I fed myself by stealing. Sometimes I walked up to a door and asked people for something to eat. Sometimes they fed me, other times they told me to get out.

If I needed something clean to wear, I snuck into someone's yard and took clothes from the clothesline. In those days, some people bathed and left their clothes by the window to air out. If I saw a shirt or a pair of pants I needed, I would grab their clothes from the window and run.

One time, a policeman saw me taking some pants, and he chased me through a neighborhood. I was running across a yard, and when I turned around to see where he was, a clothesline caught me across the neck and hooked me.

My feet went up in the air, and it felt like my skeleton was being ripped out of my body. I hit the ground, blacked out, and woke up in jail.

A lot of kids like me jumped the trains that ran through Albuquerque. Especially the Indians. We would travel the trains from town to town. I started jumping trains with Ray and Mogli, even before we went to Springer. We jumped trains to go to the fairs in Las Vegas, New Mexico. We went to the dances. We got in fights.

The one who really liked to fight was Mogli. He was a boxer. He was a good-looking kid and also a womanizer, so he was always getting into trouble and having to fight his way out of situations.

When we went to Vegas, we slept on top of the hills and cliffs around the town. We hung around with a group of guys from Roswell. They had been kicked out of Roswell, and they had wandered up to Vegas. We called them the "Joe Millers." They had funny names like "El Tiruli" and "Pintorito." We liked to party it up on the hills.

Riding the trains could be tricky. When the weather was bad we would look for boxcars, so we could stay out of the wind. But the problem was that when we were in a boxcar, we couldn't see outside.

Sometimes the railroad workers would unhook the boxcar and leave it out in the middle of nowhere. We would sit in the car waiting and waiting, and then finally we'd get out and see that the train had dropped the car, and there would be nothing around us for miles. Nothing except sky and desert.

One time, I was traveling with Ray and Mogli and another guy, and our car got dropped in the mountains near Flagstaff, Arizona. There were no stores or houses nearby, only forest, so we got out and started walking.

It was winter, and it started to snow. None of us had winter coats or good shoes. By late afternoon, it was snowing so hard we couldn't see, but we kept walking.

By evening, the snow was up to our knees, and we hadn't seen a town or house all day. We hadn't eaten, and we were cold and hungry.

Just before it got completely dark, we saw buildings up ahead of us. We walked up to them and saw that the buildings were empty. So we went up to a building that looked like a big house and broke a little window and crawled inside.

The house had a refrigerator, fireplace, and wood. The first thing we did was to light a fire. Then we went into the kitchen and helped ourselves to the canned goods.

In the morning, turkeys showed up right at the door. I went into a barn, looking for something to help me catch a turkey. I found all kinds of saddles and bridals, so they must have had horses up there in the summer. They also had bows and arrows.

I had never used a bow and arrow before, but it didn't take a sharp shooter to shoot one of the turkeys since they were just standing around. The turkey I killed had a big ol' red thing on his head.

Ray watched me kill the turkey. "Man, you're good with that bow!"

"Since I'm so good with a bow," I said, "You're going to pluck it."

So Ray plucked it, and then we took out all of the insides, and we cooked it.

We stayed there about a week until the snow subsided. Then we were able to follow a road and make our way to a town.

CHAPTER 13

A Helping Hand

When the three of us got into a town, we tried to find work doing odd jobs. Nobody's going to hire three guys together like a gang, so we always split up.

In just about every town I landed in, I would ask the people in the town, "Where's the jail?" Then, I would go to the jail and report myself to the police.

All I had to do was stand in front of the police station, looking dusty and dirty, and right away, they would throw me in jail for seventy-two hours. I just wanted to get in there to take a shower and eat. Then, after I took a shower and got out, I'd go look for work.

But it wasn't always that easy. Once, I went to a jail and the guards beat the heck out of my face and my eyes swelled up. But who was I going to tell?

When we were ready to leave town, we would meet back at the train depot and look for a train to catch. I had learned from guys in jail, not to get on a train too early. The railroad had patrols looking for people riding the trains, and if the patrols found a guy, they would crack him on the head with a club, and he would fall off the train. It was not a soft landing.

When I was in jail, I saw a lot of guys with scars. They had been hit in the head with a club and thrown off the train. But I learned from them, and I never got thrown off.

Sometimes, I found a hiding place on the train. I figured out how to put a board under the train where the wheel is, and I was skinny enough to squeeze myself in there. That way, I was able to hide from the patrols.

Other times, I hopped on the train at the last minute while they were hooking it up. It wasn't good to get on too early, but I didn't want to get on too late, either. If you try to run and catch the train while it's taking off, you're likely to lose your arm.

One afternoon, I fell asleep in a railyard, waiting to catch a train. I remember it was snowing that day. I had stolen some hotdogs and bologna from a store, and I had put the food in an old suitcase I had found in a trashcan. While I was waiting to get on the train, I sat down to rest and fell asleep.

Suddenly, I heard someone yell, "Pablo!"

I woke up to see the train leaving. So I jumped up, grabbed my suitcase, and started running next to the train. Before I jumped, I threw my suitcase onto a flatbed car. But I threw it too hard, and it went over the flatbed and fell on the other side of the tracks.

There goes all my food, I thought. But to my surprise the train stopped and backed up. As it turned out, the train was just hooking up. That gave me time to run around to the other side and grab the suitcase. The train started moving forward again, and I threw the suitcase in a second time. This time it made it in.

At that point, I was freezing cold, and the train was picking up speed. I was running as fast as I could beside the train, and I got between two train cars, and I jumped. I grabbed the edge of the flatbed and tried to pull myself up, but the flatbed was covered with a layer ice, and my hands couldn't get a grip. By that point, the train was moving fast. I held on as long as I could, but my fingers were slipping, and I knew I was going down.

Just when I thought it was all over for me, I felt someone yank me up by the back of the belt and swing me onto the flatbed. I landed and skidded across the surface, hitting my head on a railroad tie, and I blacked out.

When I came to, I saw an Indian guy sitting on the other side of the flatbed, watching me.

"Thank you," I said.

"That's cool, Bro," he said.

In those situations, we didn't talk much. The less you knew about someone, the less you could blab about later.

CHAPTER 14

1953 Chevy

A few times I went and visited my mom, just to see how she was doing. One day, when I went to visit her, I saw my neighbor, Lugie, on the porch talking to my sister.

Lugie used to be a little kid, but she had grown up while I was gone, and she had gotten pretty. So I walked over and started talking to her.

Right away she didn't like me. Lugie's father was very strict, and he didn't like me talking to his daughter, either. Well, I don't blame him. But I liked Lugie, so I started coming over and hanging out at my mom's more often.

While I was in Albuquerque, I also started hanging out with a guy we called Pidox. I would go to his place, and we would drink together. Pidox had a '53 Chevy, and one day he taught me how to start it by tearing the wires from the bottom to get the spark going.

Not long after that, Ray, Mogli, and I were hanging out in Martineztown, and we saw a 1953 Chevy, just like the one Pidox had, sitting at the curb by Longfellow Elementary.

Across the street was an apartment, and through the window, I could see the people who owned the car, sitting down to eat their supper. In those days, hardly anybody locked their houses, let alone their cars.

After looking over the car, Mogli said to me, "I'll drive it if you can start it."

"Let's go," I said.

Mogli jumped into the car, put it in neutral, and Ray and I pushed it down the street. When we were out of sight, I started it up, and we drove until it ran out of gas.

After that, we started stealing cars all the time. If we wanted to get out of town, we just went and found a car.

Around that time something happened that got me in jail. The police knew details about the event that only one other person besides me would have known about. That person was Mogli.

I knew then that Mogli had ratted me out. I didn't mind jail. It was just the idea that Mogli had ratted on me. I never put up with putting the finger at anybody.

After that, I cut Mogli loose. When I got out of jail, I just hung around with Ray and Pidox.

Not long after, I heard that Mogli had been killed in a gang fight. He was messing around with the wrong women, and some guys from Santa Fe wasted him. They shot him.

CHAPTER 15

Pidox

One night, Pidox and I were walking by a bar, and I said, "Look at those winos coming out of the bar. Do you want to do something about it?"

"Yeah," he said. "Let's go!"

So Pidox and I just piled into a group of drunks leaving a bar and beat them up. For no reason. Just because they were winos. Pidox came from a family just like mine, and he and I both shared a hatred for winos.

Another time, Pidox and I went to a dance downtown. In school, I never knew what the teacher was teaching, but I knew other things. Like I knew that when you go to a party, and you start messing with other people's girlfriends, you're going to get into trouble.

After we'd been at the party for a while, Pidox came up to me and said, "Let's go!" As we were walking out, he said, "These Indian guys are after me."

I was holding a beer bottle, barely opened, and I went out and hid myself behind the wall. A guy came out after Pidox, and I hit him with the bottle, right in the forehead.

After that a whole group of guys started after us, and we ran to Pidox's Chevy. We jumped inside and slammed the doors.

One of the guys caught up with us and punched the window on the passenger's side with his fist, shattering out the glass. Pidox put the car into gear, and we took off.

We got away that night, but the shattered-out glass left a big hole in the window of Pidox's Chevy. Pidox never did put the glass back in. Instead, he put in a piece of cardboard.

CHAPTER 16

Obscure Glass

Almost everyday, Lugie would invite me over to her house and make me a big plate of toast. Lugie's family had all the good stuff: bread, butter, jelly. They ate food like meatloaf and mashed potatoes. I had never eaten any of that.

I wanted to show Lugie how much I liked her, so I went by the cemetery in Martineztown and took a bouquet of flowers off a grave to give her. Who's going to know where they were from? I didn't tell her.

One thing I did know was that you can't take a girl out if you don't have money, and I didn't have money, so I started getting little jobs here and there. I got a job in a lumberyard. I learned how to cut glass and how to do a little carpentry. Pretty soon I got good at it. Then I started doing some work on my own. I started to settle down because of Lugie.

One afternoon, I came down with a fever, so I went to my mom's house and lay on the couch, watching TV with Lugie. Back then, we just had three channels, 4, 7, and 13. My symptoms were getting worse, so I started to think I had the flu.

By that point in my life, I was drinking sixteen ounces of turpinhydrate every day, smoking marijuana, and taking all kinds of pills. I hadn't taken any turp that day, so I thought that all I needed was a little bit of it to make me feel better.

While Lugie and I were watching TV, Pidox showed up at the house in his Chevy looking for me. He drove up outside and honked his horn. When I looked out the door and saw Pidox, I knew he would help me out with the turp. So I turned to Lugie and said, "Hey, your dad's calling you."

Lugie ran home, and I got in the car with Pidox. I told him I was sick, and he said, "Hey, I've got a friend in the Heights who will sell you the turp. He works in a drugstore."

"Let's go!" I said.

Pidox drove us up to the Heights, but he didn't go through the drive-up window at the drugstore like he should have. Instead, he drove around the drugstore. He drove around two times. I should have snapped to what he was doing, but I didn't. All I was thinking about was getting the turp.

The third time Pidox drove around the block, we saw red lights flashing behind our car. It was the jura.

Pidox pulled over to the side of the road. The policeman walked up to the driver's window and asked for Pidox's license.

"I pulled you over because of obscure glass," he said to Pidox. Then he pointed to the piece of cardboard that was in the passenger window of Pidox's Chevy. It was the same window the Indian guy had knocked out that night at the dance.

The policeman went back to his car and checked Pidox's license. During the license check, Pidox showed up as a two-time loser. That meant he had already been sentenced to prison twice. This gave the police probable cause to search the car.

The policeman came back to the car and opened the passenger door where I sat slumped down, feeling sick, not moving. He pushed me aside, bent over, and looked under my seat. He pulled out a sawed-off shotgun, a pair of nylons, and gloves.

He set aside the shotgun and then pulled out his gun and put it to my head. With his other hand, he grabbed my arm, yanked me out of the Chevy, and put Pidox and me in the back of his police car. He took us both to jail where he booked us for attempted armed robbery and sawing off a shotgun. They called it the "Fire Arm Act" in the law books.

They threw Pidox and me in the same cell. While we were waiting to see the judge, Pidox gave me his whole story.

"Eeee, I don't know what I'm going to do. My dad left us, and there's ten in the family, and nobody's there to take care of them but me."

Pidox was a two-time loser which meant that if he were sentenced to prison a third time, he would be in there for life. I hadn't been in that kind of trouble, so we both knew that if I were convicted, my sentence would be a lot shorter.

So I took the rap. They gave me five years. They let Pidox go. I think I was eighteen or nineteen at the time. I never kept up with the years. To me, one year was as good as another.

CHAPTER 17

Chains

While I was in jail in Albuquerque waiting to be sent to prison, Lugie came to visit me. She brought me some candy and cigarettes, and I shared them with my cellmate Leon. I also shared the cell with a man from Texas, an Anglo. I remember, he was lying in his bed on his side, writing a writ of habeas corpus to get out jail. He was acting as his own lawyer.

I was laying on the bottom bunk next to him, and Leon was in the top bunk above mine. As I ate my candy, I lay in bed whistling because I was happy that Lugie had come to see me. All of a sudden, the white guy called out, "Shut up!"

I started whistling louder, so he yelled at me again, "I told you to shut up!"

I got up from my bunk, walked over to his bed, and leaned down and whistled right in his ear.

He got up from his bunk to fight me, and then Leon jumped him from the top bunk. We tore up that writ of habeas corpus and made him eat it. He was yelling, "Help! Help!"

Then the guards came and got him out of our cell.

I didn't take nothing from nobody. I was in the hole, I didn't care. You show fear and you're bait. So me and Leon took care of business.

When the marshals were taking me to prison, they strapped me down in a truck with two other guys. I had a chain across my chest, a belt across my waist, and I had chains on my feet. They were taking us to *la pinta*, the federal penitentiary in Reno, Oklahoma.

I remember we were on our way out of Albuquerque, sitting at the stoplight at Central and San Mateo. I looked out the window, and I saw construction workers laying the cement for that tall bank building on the corner. I remember it, because when I came out of prison, the bank was finished.

I was strapped in the truck with Leon and an Anglo named Lo. But Lo was real homie. We didn't make it to the prison in one day, so we stopped at a jail for the night. The jail was segregated: the Blacks had their cell, the white supremacists their cell, the Indians had their cell.

But the guards threw me and Leon into the wrong cell. They put us into the cell with all the *watchos*, the Anglos. So Leon and I didn't sleep that night. He and I sat with our backs together. I sat looking this way, and he sat looking that way. We kept each other awake all night, because you don't know what's going to happen. That's how we spent our first night.

CHAPTER 18

La Pinta

The fact of prison didn't hit me until I heard those big doors close on me. BANG. When they shut, I knew I was down for a long time.

In prison, they don't just throw you in with the general population on the first day. Instead they quarantine you for thirty days. That way they can classify you.

To save money, the prison used inmates as clerical workers. The clerical workers were the same vatos doing time. They were the guys who knew how to run computers, how to run offices. The clerical workers could see all of your paperwork when you first came in, so they knew everything about you. They knew if you were a gang member, if you had money, if you had rich parents. They knew if you were an easy target. They knew.

My brothers were all well-known in the prison system in the 1950s and '60s. Richard was already in la pinta when I got there. Flo was in La Tuna, in Anthony, Texas. And my little brother Rosie was in Santa Fe. We had good reputations in prison even though we were all messed up.

When you live a life locked up or on the streets, you earn a lot of respect. So everywhere we went, in prisons, in jails, we knew everybody. They all knew us. The clerical workers were the vatos I knew. When I showed up at Reno, they spread the word. Nobody messed with me.

I was in quarantine for thirty days. During quarantine, they don't let you go to the commissary to buy toothpaste, candy, or cigarettes. The only thing they provide you with is bueglar tobacco.

Bueglar tobacco is cow manure, and that's what they give you to smoke. It stinks like heck. It's hard to take when you are used to a pack of cigarettes. Guys who are hooked on cigarettes and candy have to sit and wait for thirty days to get money from their families, so they can get their commissary when they get out of quarantine.

My brother Richard was in la pinta ahead of me, and he was already in the workforce. Several years earlier, Richard had joined the army, but while he was stationed at Ft. Bliss, they caught him dealing heroin. They sentenced him to twenty-five years in prison.

Poncho, Ray's brother, who had served time with me in Springer, was also in Reno. Poncho was the one who got his ribs broken by the guard. Richard and Poncho supplied me candy, cookies, cigarettes, joints. Whatever I needed, they sent me.

After I got out of quarantine, my brother Richard and another guy tattooed my mom's name on my arm: Juanita. We used a cactus needle, and we made ink by mixing pencil lead and cigarette ashes with water. I was the canvas. I tried to tattoo Lugie's name on my arm, too, but it went wrong. I was loaded at the time.

I never bothered anybody I knew on the outside when I was in the pen. I never called nobody. I saw guys driving themselves crazy trying to hold on to the outside. You're sitting there waiting for a letter from your girlfriend, and when you don't get it, you're wondering who's she going out with? Who's she seeing? But even if you hear that your lady is going out with another guy, what are you going to do about it? Jump the prison and see what's going on?

The way I saw it, it's better to cut everything loose. You start your own thing, and if your lady is still there when you get out, you pick up where you left off.

During those years, I never asked nobody for nothing. Nobody ever sent me letters, or money, or anything else while I was in la pinta. When I was in the cage, the outside world didn't mean nothing to me.

CHAPTER 19

Talent Scout

In prison, Poncho was what we called a talent scout. The clerical workers would tell him who the new guys were, who had money, who was weak, who could be manipulated. If a kid seemed timid or afraid or kept to himself, that kid was a done deal. He got punked out.

When Poncho came into quarantine to look around at the new guys, he already knew who the target was because the clerical workers had filled him in. He would come into quarantine while the new guy was taking a shower, and he would throw a couple of candies and a pack of cigarettes on his bed. Then he would leave.

When the guy came out of the shower, he would go to his bunk and see the candy and cigarettes. Then, he'd look around. The candy and cigarettes belonged to nobody, so he would eat it and smoke it. That would be the hook and the sinker, right there.

Poncho would give him some time, then he would come back a couple of days later and say, "Hey, how did you like the stuff?"

"Hey, it's great man. Thank you."

"Here's a list," Poncho would tell him. "I want you to fill it every week for me as soon as you get out of quarantine and start getting your money from home."

If the guy refused the list, then POP. He'd get a fist in the face.

What's he going to do? Who's he going to call? His mom? Ghostbusters? Who? So he would start filling the list. He got Poncho whatever he wanted from the commissary: candies, cigarettes, ice cream, clothes, wrist watches. Whatever they sold.

While I was still in quarantine, they put a guy from Alabama in my room with me. I had a bunk and a locker, and the guy from Alabama was right next to me. He had these funny round glasses, and he smoked the bueglar tobacco constantly in a pipe. Richard and Poncho got me the good stuff, the real cigarettes. But this guy from Alabama was smoking the cow manure, and he was killing me with the smoke.

One day I couldn't take the smell anymore, so I threw him a pack of cigarettes. He thanked me and smoked them.

Later, Poncho pulled me aside.

"You know," he said. "I have my eye on that guy. His parents are millionaires, and he's going to be getting a lot of money. Why don't you take him over?"

"I don't do stuff like that," I told Poncho. "I don't even know how."

"You already hooked him," Poncho said. "You gave him the cigarettes. He took them. Now, just slap him around a couple of times and start giving him your list."

That's how I set up the guy from Alabama. I never beat him up. I just intimidated him. I got him by the collar and told him he needed to fill my list.

At first, he told me, "I'm not going to fill any list." But, then I brought in Poncho, and a couple of other guys I knew, a black guy and an Indian.

"See those guys over there," I said.

All they had to do was to put an eye on him and after that he got me whatever I needed from the commissary. He filled my list every week. I nicknamed him "Fifi."

CHAPTER 20

Rats

On Sundays, we all used to hang around in a little park in the middle of the prison and play handball, baseball, and other activities. One Sunday, I told Fifi, "Hey, I'm having a party today, and I need you to pick up some Ritz crackers, some cookies, and some candy at the commissary."

When Fifi went to the commissary, he had to go through what we called "colored town." Everybody had their areas and you don't cross their boundaries. The Blacks sit there, the skinheads over here, the Indians over there. But the Chicanos controlled the whole prison.

After Fifi filled my commissary order, he was passing through the black section, and one of the guys grabbed his bag. When Fifi came back without a bag, I asked him, "Where's my commissary?"

"They took it from me," he said.

"Who?" I asked him. He pointed over to the black section.

So I went and got my brother Richard and los vatos, and we walked over to the black section

We went up to the guys holding the bag, and I told them it was mine. Right away they gave it back to me. We didn't have any trouble. Because the Blacks respected us. When they found out the bag was mine, they gave it back. They never bothered us. They were looking for weakness. The next time Fifi passed by them with a bag, they didn't touch him.

If we ever did have trouble, all we had to do was throw a name out—like Juan Baca.

Juan Baca was the head of the SNM, the New Mexico Syndicate. The guys in the SNM were killers. Juan Baca's gang was in every prison. Juan could walk the corridors, and he could stop someone from being stabbed to death just with his eyes. Juan could make everybody simmer down, just by his presence. He had that much power. Even the guards were afraid of Juan.

When I was going into the pen in Reno, Juan Baca was coming out. He was being transferred to another prison because he was a gang member. But his little brother was in la pinta with me. Juan grew up in Barelas, and I met his brother when they threw us in jail during los arrastres. When I was a kid, I used to hang out with the younger brothers of the Vatos Locos. They knew me. So nobody in the Syndicate messed with me.

Juan Baca told me something a long time ago. He said, "You want to run a prison. Give me at least ten guys who are not afraid to die. And I'll run the whole prison. I'll run the whole thing."

Before I got there, Juan had led prison strikes. After he left, his gang organized the strikes. If the conditions were getting bad, the gangs would form a committee and send the word out to the other inmates that they were going to lock-up the prison.

Nobody eats, nobody works, nobody goes to commissary. Before the strike, guys would start using their money to buy Ritz crackers and candy from the commissary to stock up for the strike. Then during the lock-up, we all shared. We got changes that way — more pay for our work, better food.

In prison, the gangs run things by mental violence.

I remember a guy who ratted somebody out, and they put a hit on him. In prison, they call it a "jacket." When they put a jacket on you, everybody labels you a rat. Nobody talks to you. Nobody wants anything to do with you. And when that happens, you know it's just a matter of time.

There used to be a tunnel going to the gym upstairs. In the tunnel, there was a place that was dark, before you hit the stairs. It was a small area. But if someone wanted to kill or hurt somebody, that was the spot. The guards couldn't see you.

I remember some of the inmates trapped this guy there and stabbed him in the gut. His intestines were spilled out on the floor, and guys were stepping on them as they walked by. That's what they did to guys who were rats.

They did it to send fear to the others. You see something like that and think, "Man, that could happen to me." That's what the US Army was using in Vietnam. Fear. It's all about propaganda. About showing who's stronger.

I remember a guy who was in prison for raping a little girl. They let him alone for about a year. Then, when he got comfortable and let his guard down, POP. They did away with him. They knifed him. And not just one time.

CHAPTER 21

Movidas

I didn't join the gangs when I was in la pinta. I realized that if you're a yes man, then the guards leave you alone. If you're in a gang, all the guards are going to do to you is keep you under a microscope. You can't move, you can't breathe, you can't do nothing. You're hardcore. But if you tell the prison guards "Yes, Sir," "No, Sir," then you can do your *movidas* (moves). You can do whatever you want.

I knew all the gangs. But I got along with everybody. I never had any trouble. After I got out of quarantine, I started working in the kitchen. I was making five dollars a month. I got up earlier than the rest of the population because we had to have breakfast ready—the bread, the milk, the cornflakes.

I picked up ideas in the movies, like how to sneak things out of the kitchen. At that time, a kitchen knife was going for twenty-five cartons of cigarettes. Cigarettes in those days were about twenty cents a pack, but they were used to barter, and whoever had more cigarettes was rich in prison.

In the morning, they used to bring in big cans of milk from the dairy. But there were too many in prison, and the milk didn't stretch that far, so we threw in a couple of bags of powdered milk to make it last.

Before they mixed in the powdered milk, I filled pitchers with the cream that had floated to the top of the dairy cans. Then I added some eggs to the cream and mixed it up. I sold it to the guys who were weight lifting.

I never sold it to my brother Richard. I gave it to him, but I sold it to the other guys for cigarettes and candy. I also used to make tortillas for them. I even learned how to bake bread. I learned how to do a lot of things in the prison. *Pero*, I was never under a microscope. Why fight the guards? You can't do nothing. You can't move. I liked to move.

I spent some of the money I made at my kitchen job on things at the commissary. One day, I had just made commissary. I had bought cigarettes and candy for me and Richard and some ice-cream to share with the other guys. I took everything back to the little park where Richard and the others were sitting, and right before I got there, I tripped and fell.

My bag split open and everything spilled on the ground.

Some of the guys came over to help me pick it up. While they were picking things up, out of the corner of my eye, I noticed that one of the guys, Bufa, put a pack of cigarettes under his shirt.

I didn't say anything to him at that moment. I just got everything back in my bag, and we all sat down. Then, when Bufa had settled down, and I saw him looking comfortable, I took my foot and pushed him on the shoulder, tipping him backwards.

I had learned at a very early age that if someone disrespects you or tries to intimidate you, you've got to take care of business right then and there. You don't wait. Otherwise they punk you out. And on the streets and in prison, it's very easily done.

Right away, Bufa jumped up, and then his brother, Mingo, stood up beside him. Then Richard stood up next to me, and then all the guys stood up.

But we cooled it down, because everybody knew that Bufa was in the wrong.

"Hey, man," I told him. "You don't steal from me. If you want something, ask me. I'll give it to you."

He had ripped me off. But he knew that. So he simmered down. There was no fight. But if I had let him take the cigarettes, he would have taken advantage later on.

In prison there's the law within the law. When I went to play handball, I could take off my watch and leave it on my bunkbed, and it would be there when I got back. It was the same for all the guys in my cell. And we were all thieves.

That's because in prison, there were certain lines nobody crossed. There were certain areas you couldn't tag because there would be consequences. You could lose your life if you crossed that line.

One evening, we were going up the stairs through the tunnel to go watch movies, and the guy behind me pushed me. Right away, I turned around and grabbed him and pushed him against the wall. But when he saw my face, he said, "Hey man, you know me!"

It was Russ, a guy I knew from the streets. After that, Russ and I became good friends. We used to play handball together as a team, and we won a lot of games.

Right before I got out of prison, I sold Fifi to Russ, who still had another year in. I told Fifi, "Do what Russ tells you."

When Russ got out of prison, he sold Fifi to Lugie's cousin.

CHAPTER 22

No Strings Attached

My brother Richard worked in a broom factory. He was making thirty dollars a month. At that time, they were giving six months good time to inmates who would let themselves get tested with medicines they were trying out for hepatitis and other diseases.

Richard wanted to cut down his time, so he volunteered to be a guinea pig. They put him in the hospital, and they were shooting him up with all kinds of diseases. I don't know what they were shooting him up with, but I knew I didn't want it. So I didn't volunteer.

After I had put in most of my time, they offered me parole to get out early. But I told them, "I don't want no parole. You keep your parole. I love it here. As a matter of fact, I might commit another crime if you put me on parole."

I didn't want parole because if you're even one day from finishing your parole and you blow it, you're back to the five years, or whatever your sentence is. You never finish.

I wanted to just do my time and get on. I didn't want to have to report to a parole officer. So I refused parole. I didn't want any strings attached.

CHAPTER 23

Lugie

The day I got out of prison, I hopped a bus with a friend of mine. We got off the bus in Amarillo, and the first thing we did was go get drunk. Nobody could tell me nothing. I had done all of my time.

When I got back to Albuquerque, I went to visit my mom. While I was in prison, my mom had married a guy named Manual. He was a wino. That's the way my mom survived. Because no one was giving her anything. All four of her oldest sons were in prison, and we never gave her nothing.

She didn't want me when I got out of prison. But my mom and Manuel had a little wooden shed in the back of the house next to the outhouse, and that's how I snuck back in. I slept in there one night, and they let me stay. Later, I put a mattress in the shed and a wood stove because it was winter.

I got a job at the Student Union Building at the University of New Mexico working as a busboy. I got paid fifty-seven dollars every two weeks.

One night after work, I went into the house to visit my mom and brothers. Manuel had been out drinking, and when he came in and saw me in the house with my mom and my little brother Joaquin, he started cussing and telling off my mom. He called us all *montenidos*, which means that he had to support us.

"They only come to eat and sleep!" he yelled.

When he called us montenidos, my mind went blank. All I could remember were the winos that my mom used to hang around with when I was a little kid. The ones that would throw the house and make me pee my pants.

All that came back to me, and so while Manuel was yelling, I went outside and grabbed a fence post out of the ground. I came back inside with the fencepost and swung it at Manuel and hit him in the head. Then I beat him up. I could have killed him.

My mom called the police, but Lugie saw what was going on, and she came running. She took me to her house and hid me, so the police couldn't find me.

That's when I started sleeping outside in the car. By then, I had a '52 Chevy. I parked my car outside of Lugie's house, right next to her grandmother's window, and that's where I slept.

Lugie had waited for me while I was in prison. One day, after I got paid, I asked her to marry me. I had fifty dollars in my pocket. We got married in the Catholic church. After the wedding, in the middle of the night, while she still had her wedding dress on, we went looking for a honeymoon cottage.

I knew a lady who was renting an apartment on Fifth and Menaul. It was a little place where you open the closet door and the bed is attached to the door. You flip it down. I paid this lady ten dollars for rent. That's all I had left until my next paycheck.

CHAPTER 24

My Way

About a year after we were married, Lugie and I had our first baby, Anna. By then, I was doing odd jobs here and there to support my family, but I couldn't get steady work. When I went to apply for a job, they would give me an application, but I couldn't even write my name.

I would bring the application home, and Lugie would fill it out. Where it asks if you've ever been convicted of a felony, I'd tell her, "Say no." And she'd write no. A week later, they would fire me because I had lied on the application. But if I'd tell her to write yes, then they wouldn't hire me.

After our second daughter, Joanna, was born, we needed a bigger place to live. One day, after another workplace turned me away, I got fed up, and I decided that I couldn't get a job. I couldn't read. I couldn't write. I had been in prison. So I told my wife, "If we're going to stay together, I'm going to support you my way."

That's when I started my dealings.

I started dealing heavy in marijuana and pills. I never dealt heroin. I could have, because three of my brothers were in it up to their necks. I had tried it one time with my brothers. They started me out on the *algodón*, the cotton, but I didn't like how I felt. I didn't like what it did to people. After that, I never did heroin again. I stuck to selling pills and marijuana.

I started making good money. With my earnings, we built us a brand new three-bedroom house. I used to put a big plastic bag with a pound of weed on the table. I had my daughters pull it apart and clean out the sticks, and Lugie would weigh it and bag it. Then I would go and sell it.

Guys I knew would call me, and then I would meet them places. When I took Lugie to Bingo, I would drop her off and then meet somebody and pick up some money. I was able to give Lugie a good life. She always had whatever she wanted.

At one point, I realized that if I grew my own marijuana, I could make more money. I knew guys who could read and who knew how to put things together, so I asked them to show me how to pollinate weed. If you learn something and put it into practice, you get good at it. Before long, I had my whole backyard filled with marijuana plants.

One day, I saw a guy selling a bunch of sticks. Another guy came up and told me, "That guy's got some tremendous Thai weed, man. Fifty bucks a shot."

I looked at it, and I asked, "What did you call it?"

"Thai weed," he said.

After that, I went home, and I told Lugie, "Hey! We're going to sell some Thai weed!"

All I did was tie the weed to a stick and call it "Thai weed." And they bought it. For the same price that the guy from Taiwan was selling it.

If you sell the best *mota* there is, then they're going to come. I became one of the biggest pushers of marijuana in town. I treated it like a job, like being a plumber.

I had a garage in my house with a stove and a pool table. When I harvested my *juana*, all of the buyers would come in, about five or six guys at a time, and we'd play pool.

One day, Lugie noticed some new neighbors moving in next door. She watched them move in, and then she came up to me and said, "The police have moved next door. They saw your plants. They're going to catch you and send you back to prison."

I went and looked out the window. Our new neighbor was a Spanish guy, and he had a police car parked in front of his house. His wife was Anglo, and they had a little girl. I let a few days go by, then I went over and met him. Later, I made friends with his brother. My neighbor knew about me. He knew I had all my plants back there, but he never did anything about it.

Sometimes, he would bring me weed the police had confiscated. I had a crowd in my garage all of the time, playing pool and poker, and my neighbor would walk right into my garage in his police uniform. You should have seen those guys scramble, trying to find a way out. They would try and hide, but then I'd tell them, "He's all right."

He never sold me the marijuana. He just gave it to me. He'd bring me a big bag and say, "I brought you something. Let's see if you like it."

I was making good money as a dealer, but I needed a front, so I got a job in a lumberyard. I didn't think I was going to last there, but I lasted eleven years. I went to work every day, but I was still doing the other on the side. When I left that job, I worked for several other lumberyards, and then I got a job with a freight company and stayed for seven years.

After I left the freight company, I got a job at the City working in the Weed and Litter Department. I started out working in the lowest position they had. I went out on whatever crew they sent me on.

I was working, but all the time I was still dealing. I was still messed up. Not only was I doing marijuana and pills, but I was drinking more and more. I was becoming a drunk, a wino.

CHAPTER 25

Richard

After I had gotten out of prison in Reno, my brother Richard got himself transferred to a prison in California. Richard was what we called a tourist prisoner. When he wanted to leave a place, he would get himself into trouble, and they would transfer him.

Richard kept getting himself transferred, until finally, he ended up in maximum security at McNeil Island in Washington. That's where they put the worst of the worst. At that point, Richard couldn't get himself transferred anywhere else because McNeil Island was the last prison on the line. There was nowhere else Richard could go.

While he was at McNeil Island, Richard met another inmate who used to be a lawyer. The lawyer had gotten mixed up with the mob, and that's how he landed in prison.

Richard and the lawyer became friends, and Richard told the lawyer that when he left the army, they had given him a dishonorable discharge because of his dealings. They had also given him a kangaroo court. Richard was sentenced for twenty-five years, but he had never had a fair trial.

After listening to Richard's story, the lawyer told him, "I'm going to try and get you out of here." So the lawyer wrote a petition for clemency to the attorney general, Robert Kennedy, on Richard's behalf.

But there was a problem. While Richard was waiting for a response to his petition, Robert Kennedy was assassinated. "There goes my petition," Richard thought. "Kennedy never read it."

After that, Richard forgot about his petition. But about six months later, right before his birthday, Richard was given notice that his petition had been granted.

All Richard had to do to get the petition was to sign a waiver saying that he wouldn't sue the government. Richard signed the petition, and just like that, he was released. The army gave him honorable discharge papers. They also gave him all of his army benefits back.

After spending almost half his life in the prison system, Richard was a free man. When he got out of prison, Richard moved back to Albuquerque, and he married a woman named Theresa.

On the weekends, Richard and Theresa liked to hit the bars with Lugie and I. One night we walked into a bar, and almost as soon as we walked in, this guy went at Richard. Another guy got up to jump Richard as well, but I stopped him and said, "You better stay sitting down. You don't know who you're dealing with."

I knew my brother could take care of that guy. And he did. He knocked him out with one punch. Richard and I never shied away from a fight. We liked to fight.

During the week, Richard came over almost every evening, and we sat out in the garage. We played pool and poker, and we got loaded together.

That's how we spent the 1970s.

CHAPTER 26

Victory Outreach

One day, without telling me why, Richard stopped showing up at my house. After several days of not seeing him, I said to Lugie, "Did you tell Richard not to be coming over?"

I thought maybe she was getting fed up with us.

"No," she said, "He went to a program. That's where you should be."

"What program?" I asked. "He never told me about any program."

"He's at a church, Victory Outreach. They have a men's home where he's staying."

When Lugie told me Richard was at a church, I got pissed. Right away, I told her to take me to the men's home, so I could see him.

So Lugie and I got into the car, and we drove to an old hotel on Central and Washington. Victory Outreach had converted the hotel into a men's home, and they were running an addiction recovery program. The men held car washes to help fund the program.

I parked the car and then I walked inside and found the director. I asked him a few questions, and then I told him off. I told him that they were using my brother to wash cars, to do work, all for *nada* (nothing). Then I went and got Richard and took him out of the home.

"You don't need to be with those people," I told him as we were walking out.

I dropped Lugie off, and then I drove him to see our friends. We scored, and I got him loaded. I got him all messed up again. I took him right back to our vomit.

But he had sense enough to go back. After a few days of hanging out with me, he checked himself back into the men's home.

While he was in the men's home, Richard had met a guy named Dan Sanchez, who had also gone through the program with Victory Outreach. Dan had been a heroin addict, and he had done time in prison like us. Dan worked with Victory Outreach for a time, but then he got his own ideas about how to run a program.

When Richard finished the program, Dan told Richard he wanted to start his own ministry, and he wanted Richard to come with him. So Dan and Richard started their own ministry called Barrios for Jesus. They hit the streets together ministering to addicts, street people, and prisoners.

Dan used to come to my house, looking for me. I never looked for him. He followed me all over the place trying to tell me about how God had changed his life. But I didn't want anything to do with Dan.

One day, Dan and Richard came over, and Richard said he wanted to tell me his story. I told him he could talk, but to make it quick.

CHAPTER 27

Richard's Story

Richard told me that a few years ago, he had started hanging out with an old friend, and the two of them shot up together.

But then last year, his friend converted to Christianity.

One day, after his conversion, this friend came over to Richard's house and told him, "God wants you to give your life to him."

"I'm not interested," Richard told him.

His friend left, but then he came back another day and said, "Why don't you go to church with me just one time?"

But Richard still said no.

Then his friend tried something different. "You know what?" he said. "I'll pay you to go to church. I'll give you some drugs if you'll go to a service with me."

"Oh, yeah?" Richard said.

And he went to church with this guy.

Richard told me, "I went to church, and I was sitting there listening, and the Holy Spirit touched me. But it wasn't a feeling. It was more like suddenly everything was clear to me. I could see all of the wrong that I had done, and the wrong that I was doing. And I could see the place where I was headed. I was going to destruction. Then I thought of all the people I was hurting, my mom, my kids, all my people. And I just started crying. Right there in church.

"Then, I walked up to the altar when they had the altar call, and I gave my life to the Lord."

Next, Richard told me about something that had happened to him in prison.

"When I got transferred to prison in California, the Christians had a service. Every week, I went to their service, and I listened to one song, 'Amazing Grace.' When that song was over, I got up and left.

"One morning, I was sitting at my table in the dining hall, eating breakfast. I didn't let anybody else sit at my table because I didn't want anybody around me. The other guys were afraid of me, so they left me alone.

"But this old man from the church service walked up to me anyway. This guy was a Christian, and he was in prison for bringing Mexicans into this country illegally. They gave him ten years in federal prison.

"'You know what?' he said, "The Lord sent me to tell you...'

"'Lord?' I cut him off. 'What Lord? You're in here for bringing aliens into this country. I'm not listening to you.'

"Then I told him to leave my table.

"He left, but after that, he started following me around. He kept telling me, 'God wants to save you. God is going to give you a ministry one day.'

"'Get lost,' I told him. But every time I turned around, this old man was there telling me about God. But I ignored everything he said.

"Finally, I got myself transferred to McNeil Island. That's where I met the lawyer who wrote the petition to Robert Kennedy that got me released.

"I had forgotten all about that guy telling me I was going to have a ministry until after I got converted and started Barrios for Jesus with Dan."

I listened to Richard's story, and then I told him, "You know what? Those Hallelujahs are brainwashing you."

And I kicked him out.

CHAPTER 28

Richard with a Bible

One day Richard's wife, Theresa, invited Lugie to go to church with her. "We're having a service and then we're going to eat. I'm taking the pumpkin pies. Why don't you come with me?"

"I don't know," said Lugie. She was stone Catholic, so she wasn't sure about going to church with them.

"Don't worry," Theresa told her. "We're not going to do nothing. We're just going to eat and hang out with Richard."

Lugie went with Theresa and ended up getting converted during that service. After that, Lugie kept asking me to go to church with her, but I didn't want to. Instead, I just drove her to the church and dropped her off.

A few times I went in with her just to keep her from getting mad at me. I would walk up to the door of the church, put out my joint on the steps, and then stick it in my pocket for later. I sat through the service with Lugie, but that was it.

One Saturday, I went to visit my mom. She was sitting at the kitchen table, with my little brother, Rosie. Rosie used to give my mom rings and other little presents, and they liked to drink and smoke together. My mom loved Rosie.

I sat down at the table with them, and after we'd been talking for a while, my mom looked out the window and jumped up.

"Hide everything! *¡Hay viene el predicador!* Here comes that preacher man again! Richard with a Bible."

Sure enough, we looked out the window, and here comes Richard with his Bible, talking to the neighbors, and calling out, "Jesus is the answer for the barrio!"

While she scrambled to clear the drinks off the table, I said, "Mom! You remember when the *narcos* used to attack our homes. Were you happy when they were breaking the doors and the windows looking for Richard, and they had us all handcuffed to chairs? Did you get a kick out of that?"

"No!" she said.

"At least he's trying to change his life," I told her. "At least give him the benefit of the doubt."

"I don't want to hear none of that garbage!" she said. "Get out of here!"

I tried to help Richard out a little with my mom, but I didn't want to have anything to do with Richard's crazy religion, either. "It's all malarky," I told him.

CHAPTER 29

D.O.A.

Moneywise, living was good. I had no problem with money. Lugie and my kids never lacked anything. Lugie liked going to Bingo, so I used to give her money to go to the Bingo. I never left my family without money. I always supported them.

But I was sick. I was drinking sixteen ounces of turpin-hydrate a day, and I was taking every pill you could think of: red devils, yellow jackets, Benzedrine. Whatever got me high. Black beauties. Narcotic pills. I even took birth control pills. I didn't care. If you have a friend and he gives you a pill, are you going to check to see if it's government inspected? You just take it. Nobody analyzes the pill.

Day by day, I was getting skinnier and skinnier. Sicker and sicker. I was up to smoking about forty joints every day.

Smoking weed was the only thing that got me hungry, but even when I ate, I couldn't keep the food down.

One day, Lugie took me to a curandera in Los Lunas. This lady lived by the railroad track. Curanderas were doctors at their own risk — they didn't have a license. But for twelve bucks, this lady healed me. She turned my esophagus around, and I was able to keep down what I was eating.

But after I got healed, I still kept on doing my own movida. Joints. Pills. Three packs of cigarettes a day. I drank like a fish. I used to work with a guy named Tom Bozo. After work, I went to his house to get loaded. We smoked marijuana and we drank. Tom was a snake charmer. He raised pythons, those big snakes that wrap around you. He had about two or three in his house. I don't know how I ever got home in my truck at night after I partied at his house.

One morning, I couldn't get up for work. I had lived my life kind of loosely, but I had never cheated on the job. I had never missed work. Sick, hung-over, whatever, I still showed up. But that morning I couldn't get up.

Lugie came into the bedroom and found me lying on the floor beside the bed, curled up like a snake. I was babbling, and she couldn't make sense of what I was saying, so she called the ambulance.

The paramedics showed up and Lugie watched them put me on a stretcher and load me into the ambulance. She didn't go with me because she had to stay home with our two daughters and our nine-month-old son, Pablito, Jr.

The ambulance took me to Anna Kaseman Hospital. The paramedics carried me into the emergency room where they checked my vital signs. There were none. My heart had stopped beating. I had stopped breathing. They pronounced me D.O.A. — dead on arrival.

CHAPTER 30

Twilight Zone

I don't remember the trip to the hospital, but I remember waking up in the emergency room. What was strange was that I wasn't in my own body. Instead, I was floating in the corner of the room, and I was watching two guys come into the room and charge me up. They were trying to bring me back from the dead.

I remember seeing myself bounce up off the table. I didn't want to come back to my body because I felt good up there in the corner. I had never felt peace like I did then. I didn't have no cravings for drugs or nada. It was just like I melted down.

I didn't see them bring me back, but I knew when I came back because I could feel my body again.

The doctors diagnosed me with an ulcer and did surgery on my stomach. After that they kept me in the hospital for a few days. I remember calling Lugie and telling her I had died for a little while.

Nothing about almost dying changed me. I never thought about my out-of-body experience or why I saw myself lying dead. I didn't connect it to an afterlife, or a message from God, or anything else. I just thought I had had a crazy trip. Like I was in the Twilight Zone.

When I came out of the hospital, I went right back to my established business of selling. I went back to everything I was doing before.

But I was really low at that point. Mentally and physically I was worn out.

One evening, I was lying in my recliner in my living room, and I realized that I couldn't go on anymore. I just had to believe in something. That's when I asked God to come into my life. I told him to salvage whatever he could salvage.

The next time Lugie went to church, I went with her. When they did the altar call, I went up to the altar, and I knelt down and asked the Lord to help me. I told him I couldn't do it on my own anymore.

"If you're for reals," I told him, "I don't want no drugs no more. I don't want no calls for drugs. I don't want nobody to call me at home."

Up to that point, I was heavy into selling. I used to get calls every day, every minute from people wanting to buy something. After I went home that day, I never got another call again for drugs. Not once. I hadn't gotten the word out, but still, I never got another call. I never got a visit. I never had nobody stop by to see if I had marijuana. And they used to line up at my house like they were going to the market. It all stopped completely.

I stopped cultivating my plants. I didn't plant no more. I didn't have a desire for it no more. And I never went back to it.

I never craved another joint, another pill, another drink. It's been almost thirty-five years. I haven't had a craving for nothing. No smoking, no drinking, no nada. Nothing. The Lord was my healer and my antidote.

CHAPTER 31

Barrios for Jesus

After my conversion, I joined Richard and Dan with Barrios for Jesus. Dan was our pastor.

I went with Dan and Richard to San Antonio and learned from guys like Nicki Cruz, Sonny Arguinzoni, and Freddy Garcia. These guys were former gang members. They had been with all the old gangs. Nicki Cruz had been with the Mao Maos in New York. Sonny Arguinzoni had started Victory Outreach in California and spread it all over.

Back in Albuquerque I went out into the streets with Dan, Richard, and other guys who had joined Barrios. We went to where the hobos and winos were, under bridges, in the streets. We took them sandwiches, and we talked to them about the Lord. We went into the neighborhoods, the churches, and the prisons.

One day, Dan took us to a church called the Potter's House. I was standing in the parking lot with Richard, Dan, and all the other vatos, and we got into a circle to pray before we went inside. While we were praying, a guy came out of the church. He must have had words with the pastor because when he came out, he was pissed.

He took one look at us standing in the ring with our heads bowed, and then he picked up into a run and came straight at us. Before I could get out of his way, he kicked me. In the front. Right in the groin.

I don't know why he attacked me. He could have taken on another guy who was bigger than me. He could have gone after Richard. They all looked like notorious vatos. But he came and kicked me. Thankfully, some way or other, God protected me. I didn't go down or nothing.

After he kicked me, I didn't fight him. Instead, I grabbed my Bible, and I said, "Hey Bro, I handled your kick, can you handle my God?"

This guy was a pusher, but after that, he and I became best friends. We started praying and talking about the Lord together. He was a butcher. He used to bring me steaks.

CHAPTER 32

The Rock

Barrios for Jesus didn't have a building, so we set up tents in the parks in Albuquerque and held revivals. After we hit all of the Albuquerque parks, we started roaming the state. We went to small towns in New Mexico like Bernalillo, Tucumcari, and Belen.

One time, we went all the way to Española and put up a tent at a strip mall called "The Rock." We held a revival at The Rock and invited all the drug addicts. We played music, and all the addicts started showing up to hear the music.

After listening to the music, they prayed with us. We set up every night, and they kept coming back. After a few services, they started leaving behind their knives, guns, marijuana, and all of their paraphernalia.

Mike Naranjo was a musician in Española. He used to play the bars, and he had also been on drugs, but recently he had joined a church. One evening, he and his wife, Gloria, were coming out of a store in the strip mall when they saw our tents lit up and heard all of the praying, music, and hallelujahs coming from inside.

Mike and Gloria decided to come into the tent to see what we were all about. When Mike sat down, he saw Harry, another guy from his barrio, kneeling down at the altar praying with Dan. Harry and Mike were from the same neighborhood, but they weren't friends. They were rivals, enemies. Harry had wanted to kill Mike at one time.

Harry was kneeling down at the altar because he had just accepted the Lord. While Harry was still at the altar, he saw Mike sitting there, and he stood up and went straight for him.

Right away, Mike stood up and told his wife to stand back. Harry grabbed Mike, but instead of fighting him, he pulled Mike to him, gave him a big hug, and told him he loved him.

After that, Mike started working with us. The pastor of the church Mike was going to didn't believe in the kind of outreach we were doing, so Mike joined us. Mike lived in a trailer park, and we used to bring guys in from Albuquerque and pan the area. We handed out tracks to the neighbors and talked to them about the Lord.

We wanted to open a Barrios for Jesus in Española, so we had a meeting with Mike. But Mike told us that he didn't want to start a Barrios for Jesus. Instead, he wanted to have his own ministry. I remember Dan told Mike, "If you don't open under our name, you can't do it."

I got up and told Dan, "Why not? Mike can do whatever he wants. This is his barrio. Why do you want to infringe on his turf? Let him open something."

So we didn't open a Barrios for Jesus in Española. Instead, Mike started his own ministry called "The Rock." They built a big church. They bought an old motel and turned it into a school for kids and a center that runs programs for addicts. It's called Rock Outreach, Christian Center. Mike's ministry is doing a lot of good in Española today.

One day, I got a call from Mike to see if I wanted to bring the message over there. After I agreed, he announced to the men that Pablo Lucero was coming to speak.

Somehow, Tom Bozo, the guy with the pythons I used to party with, ended up in one of Mike's programs in Española. When he heard the name Pablo Lucero, he said, "I used to work with a guy named Pablo Lucero. You're talking about Pablo Lucero from Albuquerque?"

"Yeah, he's a pastor now," Mike told him.

"It can't be the same Pablo Lucero I knew," Tom said. "The Pablo I knew was all messed up."

But it was me.

Tom graduated from Mike's program, and he also became a pastor. Now he has a church in Rio Rancho. He's a beautiful man of God.

CHAPTER 33

The Last Resort

When we went into the prisons and into the barrio, my pastor, Dan, would assign guys to preach. There were other guys with us, who were also from the barrio. They too had lived a crazy life. Sometimes a guy would say he would be there to preach, but then he wouldn't show up. Dan needed somebody to fill the gaps. He knew that I'd be there, so he would tell me, "Pablo, you know what? I'm going to use you as a last resort."

I didn't know how to read or write, but everybody knew me. I used to go into the barrio in my 1948 Chevy and all the neighbors would recognize me. They would show up to the services because they knew me. And whenever we went to the prisons, I was there.

A lot of the inmates had gone to Springer, to la pinta, and I knew them all. A lot of them I used to sell to. They all knew that I had been one of the biggest pushers of marijuana in the city, and the word spread. When I showed up at the prison, they wanted to know why I had changed. They wanted to know how that had happened.

But Dan would tell me, "If you go to prison, Pablo, and the guy who's supposed to preach shows up, then you just step away and let him do it."

One day Lugie said to me, "Why do you let Dan talk to you that way? What's 'the last resort' mean?"

I never snapped about what Dan meant by using me as a last resort. I was just glad to be used, so I told Lugie, "I'm not working for Dan as a last resort, or whatever he calls it. I'm doing this because of what God did for me. An opportunity is an opportunity no matter how it comes up, and I'm an opportunist. If they give me a few minutes to preach here and there, I'll take it."

CHAPTER 34

A New Supervisor

After I joined Barrios, I was still working with the city. One day, my supervisor sent me to take a weed eater to a shop to get it repaired. I took it into the shop, dropped it off at the counter, and then went back outside. But instead of waiting in my truck, I snuck around behind the shop and watched the guy through the fence to see how he fixed it.

All he did was take the nut from the top and close it, and he charged the city thirty-five dollars. I went back to my supervisor, and I said, "Hey, Al, these people are ripping you off over there. Why don't you let me take care of the weed eaters? I'll fix them. I know how to do it."

So he put me in charge of fixing the weed eaters. After that, I learned how to fix a lot of other tools instead of taking them to the shop. I started saving the city *feria* (money) that way. Later my supervisor gave me an office, and I maintained the tools and handed them out to the guys.

But then my supervisor, Al, left. We got a new supervisor, but the new supervisor took a dislike to me. I knew his people. I knew where he came from. He came from the barrio like me, and he was an addict. He had a bad mouth, and he would cuss at his workers.

He would take a guy into his office, and then he would take this big ring off his finger and set it on his desk, like he was going to beat the guy up. Every time, the guy would come out of his office blubbering.

One day he tried the same thing on me. I could tell by the way he talked to me one morning what was going to happen, so before he could call me in, I walked into his office.

I locked the door behind me, and I said, "Take off your ring, or your watch, or whatever you're going to take off because me and you are going to throw this office. I'm going to mop the floor with you."

He started screaming, "What do you mean trying to intimidate me? You can't talk to me that way! I'm your supervisor!"

But after that, he didn't mess with me. I did whatever I wanted. Because he knew where I was from.

But he figured out how to do me harm in other ways.

CHAPTER 35

Community Service

The first thing my supervisor did was to move me out of the tool room into a supply closet where they keep all the chemicals and the gasoline. The city policy is that you have to have the chemicals away from people. But in the closet where he moved me, the chemicals and the gasoline cans were all stacked behind my desk. Then he took away my work truck, and he changed my job.

He put me in charge of the community service workers who were picking up trash by the side of the road. These were people who were doing service for things like shoplifting and DWI. I had to tell them what to do, when to get down, to clean, to do this, to do that. But I'm not a cop and that wasn't my job description.

I could have gone to the supervisor of my supervisor, because I knew him. He and I went way back. But I didn't go crying to anybody. Instead, I did the job my supervisor assigned me.

But I did it my way. I didn't just stand around giving orders to the workers. I worked with them. If they got a shovel, I got a shovel. If they picked weeds, I picked weeds. If they picked paper, I picked paper. And I was their supervisor.

They used to ask me, "How come you're doing our work?" And I would say, "Well, I'm no better than you, Bro. I've been where you're at. Let's go. Let's do the job and get out of here."

I never worked the girls picking up paper or weeds. I knew the superintendent in charge of the women, Benina, and I told her why.

"You get a girl, maybe in shorts, picking up weeds and papers, and there will be about ten guys over there in the back, standing around watching her. There is no work being done. So I'm going to use a little wisdom: eliminate the candy, and they gotta work."

I signed the women in, and then I took them out and bought them a cup of coffee and a donut. I kept them for about half an hour, preached to them, and then signed them out and let them go home.

The guys asked me, "What are you doing with the women?" And I told them, "You can't handle the one you got at home. How are you gonna handle this one? Go do your work over there, man."

But I used to help a lot of the guys, too.

One of the workers was from Mexico. One day, he came to me and asked me for two days off, so he could go see his mother who was sick. We had a deadline to meet, so I couldn't just let him off.

He had come with his brother to talk to me, so I said, "I'll tell you what. I'll work your brother with you today, and his work will count for your second day. That way you can leave tomorrow to go see your mom."

He and his brother both worked that day, and then they went to see their mom.

Another guy from Mexico, Jorge, was also doing community service with me. Jorge came to work every day, drunk. He was a wino. So I took him under my wing and shared my story with him.

I put a microwave and a coffee machine in my little office, and I held Bible studies for guys. I invited Jorge to the Bible studies, and he started coming. He gave up drinking and changed his life, and he too became a pastor. Now he has his own church on West Central.

My supervisor tried to hurt me, but I outdid him. I got to be good friends with all of the people I was supervising. I knew them all.

Once I took a busload of workers over to a convenience store after they had been working all morning, so they could go get a drink and a snack. We only allowed one guy at a time go in, because if we sent them all in, they were going to steal.

I sent the first guy in with some money, but he came back right away. He said, "Pablo, they threw me out. They wouldn't even let me in."

So I got up, and I said to all the guys, "All of you, we got work to do. Everybody, get in there."

And they did. They came out with cigarettes, candy they never paid for. They ripped the whole store off. I didn't care. That's because they treated one of the guys bad. He had money, but they wouldn't let him in.

CHAPTER 36

Insubordination

My supervisor was still out to get me, so one day he brought me two inmates from the jail. He told me that in addition to the community service workers, I was going to be supervising the ones who were locked up. They were going to release guys from jail for job detail.

Two guards were standing with them. "Here are the guards you're going to be working with," he told me. "You're going to be the supervisor. If one of the inmates gets out of hand, you just get his picture and give it to the tracker, and they'll come and take him back to jail."

"I'm not going to do that," I said.

"You better, or I'll get you for insubordination," he told me.

"I'm not going to do that," I said. "I'm not a rat like you. I'm not going to rat on anybody. And besides, are you going to help me if one of the inmates decides to hit me over the head with a shovel because I ain't got no authority? Are you going to take care of my family? I'm not that dumb, Bro.

"But I'll tell you what, since you've threatened me with insubordination, why don't you let me have that badge, and I'll gladly do it."

"Well, we can't give you a badge because you're not qualified."

"Then let's go," I told him. "Take me to insubordination."

So we went to the meeting with his supervisors to talk about my insubordination. But I knew the superintendent of superintendents, Gene Romo. Gene ran the community center in Martinez when I was growing up. He and his wife had an apartment there, and he knew all of the kids in the neighborhood. He was like a brother to me.

I had never told him what my supervisor was doing to me because I'm not a rat. I take it with a lump. But when my supervisor took me over there to his office, I told Gene what was going on. And Gene told my supervisor, "You give Pablo back his status. You give him back his truck. Then after that, you go. You're fired!"

Instead of firing me, they fired my supervisor.

And from there, I ran the whole show. I still worked with the community service workers, but I got my truck back, and I got some people to help me.

They assigned me a new supervisor at the city, and one day he called me in. He handed me a set of keys and asked me if I wanted to be a foreman.

Right away, I threw the keys back on his desk, and I told him, "I'm leaving the city, man."

"Why?" he asked.

"I've never been an informer!" I told him.

When he said the word *foreman*, I thought he was asking me to be an informant, to put the finger on the guys who weren't doing their job. That's why I told him, no.

But then he said, "Not an *informer*. A supervisor!"

I took the job, and that's how I became a foreman.

CHAPTER 37

How to Fight Crime

Not long after I became a foreman, I went to a mayor's meeting downtown with some of the guys from the department where I worked. I was sitting there with my Bible, and the mayor asked us if anybody had any input on how to stop crime in the city.

I didn't know what the word *input* meant. I thought the mayor was cussing. So I asked the guy next to me, "What's *input*, man?"

"It means, do you got any suggestions."

I stood up with my Bible, and I said, "I got one."

"Who are you?" the mayor asked.

"I work for the city," I said. "I work for the Weed and Litter Department. I'm a supervisor." Then I said, "You want to know how to fight crime in this city?"

"How?" he asked.

"Give me one of those boarded up buildings you got. And I'll show you how to fight crime in the city."

The mayor looked at the Bible I was holding, and he said, "If you're going to talk about God, we can't do that here. We need to separate church from state."

"Hey, Mayor. You've got money in your pocket?" I asked. "Yeah."

"Well, check it out. It says, 'In God We Trust.' How do you separate that? You're using God's money, but you're saying there's no God. You give me one of those boarded up buildings, and I'll make a men's home out of it. I'll take in all of those guys who are drug addicts. Crime would subside in your barrio because they would receive Christ."

They threw me out of the meeting.

CHAPTER 38

A Men's Home

Dan and Richard and I wanted to start a men's home with Barrios. A guy named Andy Barela ran a methadone center downtown. Andy knew that we were looking for a building, so he told us about a black man who had a building near Atrisco. It used to be a church, but the front had caved in.

He took us to see it, and we said, "You're crazy, man. That building's all torn up." It was just a pile of rubble, and the city had never cleaned it up. But this man said he'd rent it to us. He gave it to us for one dollar a year.

Some of the guys in Barrios knew how to throw things together, so we took the building and rebuilt it. A neighbor behind us let us hook up to his electricity with a cord, so we had lights. We had services. Our neighbors were bootleggers on one side, and drug addicts on another.

We rebuilt that church, and we turned it into a men's home. Men who were addicts would come and stay with us, and we would minister to them. The men lived there. They prayed there. They went to church there.

If a guy had been a drug addict for ten years, we didn't expect him to get well in three or four days. God tells us that we're like plants. We need to be rooted. So you stay with a guy until he's rooted. And while you're waiting for him to get rooted, you've got to thin the weeds.

When they first came to the house we would put them through a Bible study program to root them in God's Word. Everyday. Bible study, Bible study. Then cleaning, feeding. We used to sleep there with them. We would talk with them. Pray with them. Take care of them.

We did that every day until they got the *onda* (wave). Until they graduated. Then we would help them get work.

They couldn't dispute what we were saying to them because we had been where they had been. Prison is prison. A dungeon is a dungeon, and we'd been there. Beat up and tore up on the floor.

After a guy had finished the program, after he had been ministered to and was rooted in the word of God, then we would send him out to make a new life for himself and his people, for his wife and his kids. And he's not going back.

Some of them would go out and minister with us to other addicts. Some of them became pastors. We had an overflow of guys. Later we started a women's home, but we kept the men and women separate.

We had a guy from Arkansas come to one of our services. His name was Joe, and the mafia had a hit on him. Joe told us he had gone to hide out in California, carrying five-thousand dollars in one boot and five-thousand in the other. While he was there, Joe found a job working on a tugboat. Tugboats help to direct and stabilize the big ships.

One night, Joe had gone to sleep in his bunkbed on the tugboat, and the guy who was supposed to be keeping watch on deck fell asleep.

While they were all sleeping, a wave came and flipped the tugboat, tipping the whole crew into the sea.

As Joe slid off the deck, a hook caught him and cut him across the chest, making him bleed like a stuck pig. When he fell into the water, his blood attracted the sharks. The sharks swarmed the crew and ate everybody but him.

"That's when I received the Lord," Joe told us.

The first time Joe came to Barrios, I didn't know him, but for some reason he got attached to me. He needed a place to stay, and Dan told him, "Well, we ain't got money for a hotel, but you can stay at the home for men."

"No," he said. "I'm going to stay with Pablo."

So Joe started staying with me and Lugie when he came into town. I had a shar-pei dog, one of those wrinkly dogs, and I used to put a scarf around his neck. One day Joe saw my dog sitting outside, and he said, "What's that ugly thing?"

"That's a dog!" I said. "Do you want him?"

"Yeah!" he said. And he took my dog with him on his next trip to Arkansas. Joe put a red tie on him, sunglasses, and a little hat. The dog sat in the front seat.

"Man, what an ugly thing that is!" people would say.

"That's my wife," Joe would tell them.

Joe got away from the mafia. Later he became a pastor, and he married a beautiful lady. He and I used to go into the prisons and minister together.

CHAPTER 39

Florencio

My brother Florencio had gotten out of prison, but he was still into drugs. Richard and I tried to tell him our story, but he didn't want to talk about it when we came over to see him.

"You've got three minutes," he would tell us. "If you want to talk more than that, then get out of here."

After a while, he didn't even let us in his house.

Florencio got a temporary job working for the city in the Civic Auditorium where they had fights and wrestling. At that time, it was up there on the hill, where Albuquerque High School was, and they decided to tear it down.

When they tore it down, Florencio took the auditorium chairs they were taking out of the building, and he sold them. He also sold the oak floors and everything else that had any value.

But then he got caught. They busted him for theft, and they threw him into jail. He was looking at a lot of years in prison.

Dan, Richard, and I bonded Flo out, and while he was waiting for court, Flo decided to go into our program. We put him in our men's home, and he stayed with it.

When we were living the crazy life, Flo *tenia palabra*—he had word. That meant that when he gave his word, he didn't go back on it. Flo was never into conversation. His *yes* was *yes*, and his *no* was *no*. He gave his word to Dan that he would stay in the home and that was it. End of story.

After he finished the program, he never went back to smoking, drinking, drugs, heroin. Nada. Nothing.

We prayed for Flo, and we made a petition in court for him because he had successfully made it through our program. Some of the judges knew our program because we used to go to court with the guys in our program.

When we presented our program to the judges, we told them, "This guy isn't going to change in prison. Why don't you give him a shot with us? We'll be responsible for him."

So the judges worked with us. They didn't want to waste the taxpayer's money on keeping some yoko in there for thousands of dollars. And we didn't charge the state nothing.

We made our petition on Flo's behalf, and we talked to the judge and told him that Flo had made it through our program. The judge ended up letting Flo go.

After that, Flo got a job as a welder at the Rio Grande Steel company, and he became one of their best welders. He retired from there. Flo has always been a good husband, a good father. Today, he's eighty years old, and he still lifts weights. Flo and his wife, Lillian, get up every morning and clean offices.

Flo still dresses sharp. Now, he'll give you the shirt off his back. Somebody came up to me the other day, and said, "Look what Flo gave me, man!" This guy was wearing some nice pants. They were expensive clothes that Flo gave him.

CHAPTER 40

Breakup

After I had been working with Barrios for five or six years, my pastor Dan fell. We didn't know the details. It wasn't drugs, but he had gotten back into the world, and we all knew because he wasn't the same.

He told us one day that he couldn't act as our pastor anymore. So he left Barrios, and he went to be restored with Sonny Arguinzoni at a Victory Outreach home in California.

When we had started Barrios for Jesus, we made bylaws. The bylaws said that if the head guy fell, then he would give the mantel to the next guy who was faithful. And then that guy would take the lead and keep it going. If you drop the flag, then somebody else is going to pick it up, like in the army.

When Dan fell, everybody expected that the ministry was coming to Richard or me because we were next in line. But when Dan left for California, he gave his position as lead pastor to his son, Danny, Jr. He didn't pass it on to one of us.

Danny, Jr. was a good guy, but he had never worked the streets. He had never been in prison. He'd never been beat up in the dark. He had never been a drug addict. He was a fireman.

But we didn't fight with him about it. We let him take leadership. But then Danny, Jr. transferred Barrios for Jesus back to Victory Outreach. He gave Victory Outreach the church and the men and women's home.

All of a sudden, we were no longer Barrios for Jesus. We were Victory Outreach. A lot of the people in Barrios went back to Victory Outreach with Danny. He was a wonderful pastor, but he was Victory Outreach.

And I didn't want to join with Victory Outreach.

My brothers Flo and Richard, my friend Eddie and a few others didn't transfer back to Victory Outreach, either. We didn't join with them because we didn't agree with their way of organizing the ministry. At Victory Outreach the head guys don't let outsiders preach.

The way we looked at it, if somebody pops up who has a relationship with the Lord, then he might have an answer for other people, so we let him preach. We're not going to check his credentials. If he's got a word that God gave him, then he should spit it out.

If he's of God, then he's going to last, and God will bring him people to minister to. If he's not of God, then he's going to fizzle out. That's how we tell if he's from God, by his fruits.

But Victory Outreach didn't see things that way.

After Barrios broke up, I told Lugie, "I don't know what to do, now. I don't have a church place. I don't have no community. I feel like all my time building up Barrios was wasted."

Lugie listened to me, and then she said, "Pablo, when you almost died in the hospital, I was worried about you. So I went to the pastor's wife, and she told me to pray for you. After that, every time I was with you, I prayed. And things changed for you. Why don't you pray?"

So I started going to a pancake house every morning before work, and I studied my Bible.

Each morning, I opened the Bible and looked at the words, and the Lord started teaching me his message. I still don't know a lot of words, but when I open the Bible, I look for the words I know, and then I see pictures. I picture the people and the culture like I'm watching a movie.

People asked me, how did you find this or that out? I tell them, "God taught me. He's showing me every time I open the Bible."

For example, when I got to the part in the Bible where Jesus talked about salt, I imagined the scene. I could see

Jesus studying the salt and then telling people to be the salt of the earth.

When we lived in the mountains, my dad and my grandpa cured deer meat with salt. That's how we preserved the meat and kept it from rotting. That's the same way they used salt in the Bible, to preserve the meat. Also, salt gives flavor to your food. And salt also makes you thirsty.

I pictured the scene, and then I asked God, "What does that mean that we're to be salt?"

He told me, "You've got to be like the salt if you follow me. You're a preservative, because you don't fight no more. You fight with the Word. You don't want to hurt nobody no more. Instead, you help people.

"Salt makes people thirsty, and people thirst for the kind of life you live now. You treat people with respect, so you give flavor to them wherever you go."

CHAPTER 41

Ticket to Nebraska

One morning, I was sitting in the restaurant reading my Bible, and this young guy came in the door messed up y todo. Right away the boss went running and told him "Hey, get out of here!"

I called out to the guy, "Come on over here, man!"

The guy walked over to my table. "They don't want me in here."

"They won't throw you out," I told him. "You're with me. Sit down."

He sat down, and I asked him, "Do you want to eat? Order whatever you want. I'll pay for it."

He ordered some food, and we talked while he was eating. He told me he was from Nebraska, and he wanted to go back home.

After he finished eating, I took him to the bus station, and I bought him a ticket to Nebraska. He was crying when I gave him the ticket. He said, "How come you're doing this?"

"I've been where you're at, man," I said. "I know how it is to get up in the morning by the bus stop and take a newspaper and use it as a blanket. You wake up cold and stiff. I know how it is to sleep under a bridge. I know how to eat roadkill. I know how it is when nobody gives you a hand. I've been there, man."

He left Albuquerque. He went happy. We cried together, and he left.

That's the way it is in prison, too. You've got bros. You've got homies. We tell each other, "Hey, I knew your brother, man. If you need anything, just send me a kite. I'll take care of it." So why can't we help each other like that out of prison?

Another time, while I was sitting in the restaurant, my wife's brother-in-law came in. He had been to Vietnam, and he and I used to play poker and drink together. We were good friends. But after I converted, we didn't get to talk too much.

When he came into the restaurant he saw me at a table reading, and he asked if he could sit down with me. I said, "Yeah. Come on."

He sat down and asked me what I was doing. I told him I was reading the Bible, and he asked me what I was reading.

I told him I was reading John 3:3 where Jesus is telling Nicodemus that he must be born again.

"I'm getting out of here," he said. "All you talk about is the Catholics. That's why I don't hang around with you, anymore. That's all you talk about. You put them down."

"I didn't mention no Catholics," I said.

"I go to San Martin," he said. "I'm an altar boy there. I help the priest. And you're always talking about the Catholics."

"Well, you have a Bible this big, don't you?" I said. "I've seen them. It takes two of you to put it in the pulpit. Open that book, man. John 3:3. It'll tell you the same thing this small book will tell you. You must be born again. It has nothing to do with being Catholic. It doesn't have to do with religion. It has to do with a relationship with the Lord."

He got pissed at me and he left.

CHAPTER 42

How Many Rats?

Even though I didn't have a church, I kept going into the prisons. By the time Barrios ended, I was going to la pinta in Santa Fe and the Santa Fe jail. I also went to the prison in Grants, and I went to Rio Rancho and the Westside in Albuquerque. I went all the way to Hobbs and Cruces. I hit every pinta I could think of.

When I went to give a service in the prison, I would look at the inmates, sitting there all tagged down, mean looking, y todo. And I would say, "Hey! The first thing I want to know, man, is how many rats are here? You know, snitches. Can you raise up your hand, man?"

When I asked that question, nobody's hand would go up.

And then I would say, "I'm going to prove to you that we're all snitches."

I said to one guy, "What's your name?"

"Pepe Sanchez!" he called out.

"Pepe, you mean to tell me, if they broke into your house, you wouldn't call the police?"

"*Chale!* I don't call the cops on nobody, man!"

"Well, I know why."

"Why?"

"Because everything you got is stolen. You don't have no paper for the TV, the computer, or anything else that you got at your house. Not even your clothes. You don't got no proof that it's yours. That's why you don't call the police.

"But tell me this, say that you get out of here, and you buy a little car, and you get insurance. Say that somebody comes and hits you in the back. You didn't get hurt or nothing, but how come you call the police on them? It's the same police they use on you? So how come you're ratting these people out?

"How come you don't just take your dented car and just say, 'Bye. Go on'? Because you want the money, right? You want the insurance money. See, you want to use the system when it's to your advantage. But you're still a rat. So why don't you kill yourself?"

If you go to prison and somebody puts the finger on you that you're a rat, they'll kill you. Sooner or later. So I tried to get the inmates to look at rats from a different perspective, because everybody's like that when it's to their advantage.

CHAPTER 43

Who Do You Follow?

Every week, I used to go downtown to the jail in Albuquerque. They call it the Three Norths. Once, this guy who drove a motorcycle invited me to go with him into the prisons. We met in the parking lot of the jail downtown, and he told me, "You don't know these people you're going to be dealing with. You follow my lead."

But as soon as we went in there, they all knew me.

"Oh, you've been here?" he asked me.

"Yeah. I'm the one that broke the ground over here," I told him. "All these friends I know from the streets."

In Three Norths, they have an upstairs called the Details for the guys who are out of it. The guys in the Details wear only boxers. They aren't allowed to wear belts. When you walk by, they spit at you, throw fingers, cuss.

When I first started preaching there, I remember I was standing on the ground floor, and the guard handed me the microphone and told me to talk to the Detail inmates from downstairs.

"If you're going to give a service here, then you have to use the microphone. I can't let you go up there because of the way they are," he told me.

I handed him back the microphone and said, "I'm not going to preach using this. I'm going to go upstairs."

"It's not safe for you to go up there," he said.

"I feel safer with them up there than with you down here," I told him.

So he let me go. I took my Bible with me. One guy was standing at the door of his cell in his Fruit of the Looms, screaming and cussing. When he saw me, he stopped yelling and said, "Hey! Pablo. What's going on?"

I happened to know him. I had married him and his wife. We went way back.

I knew a lot of guys that were there. The guards were amazed when these guys stopped cussing and throwing fingers. I talked to the guys, and they respected me because they knew me. I came back many times after that to work with them.

I would go into their cells and sit and talk with them. In every cell I went, I saw a picture on the wall. I would look around and there would be a picture of Al Capone. So I knew this guy was following Al Capone.

Al Capone was a mighty killer. He was this guy's model. Al Capone was the one he wanted to be like. The Mexicans had a picture of Zapata that said, "*¡Viva Zapata!*" (Long live Zapata!) in honor of the uprising in Mexico. So I knew they followed Zapata. The bald-headed guy would have a picture of a swastika. He followed Hitler.

I noticed all of these things, and I asked God about it, and he told me what to do. The next time I went into a cell, I pointed at a poster, and I asked the guy I was visiting, "Who's that?"

"That's Al Capone!"

"You know something?" I said. "I'm going to tell you the truth. I've been around a long time, and Al Capone is dead. He died from syphilis in the head. You can go to his grave and dig up his body. You see that Hitler? He's dead, also. He committed suicide. His grave is still there. And Zapata? He got killed, too. All these guys, you can go to their coffins, and they're still there.

"But the man I serve, you can go to his grave, and he's not there. Because he's a resurrected man. He's still alive. That's the one I serve, and that's the one that cleansed me. Not a program, not the prisons, not the parole office, not the methadone, none of that. I just surrendered to him, and I try to do the best I can with his help.

"Al Capone, that man is dead. Hitler is dead. Zapata is dead. But go to the one I'm talking about, and you won't find him. He's resurrected, man. And he lives in you, if you want him."

CHAPTER 44

Spit-Out Nails

One time I went to Three North with a younger guy who was interested in the ministry. I was getting ready to lead a service downstairs, and one of the guys from the Details started walking down the metal stairs, making a lot of noise with his feet. The guys were already sitting there waiting, and so I started the prayer to begin the service.

While I was praying, the guy from the Details finished walking down the stairs. But instead of sitting down with the others, he came up to the front where I was standing. My head was bowed, and he walked up to me, grabbed me by the shoulder, and spun me around. Then he pushed me.

I stopped praying, and I turned around and looked up at this guy. He was mean-looking. He had scars all over his face, no teeth. And he was big.

"You ain't preaching over here," he told me.

"Why not, man?"

"Because you're not a Catholic."

"I am a Catholic," I said. "And I'll die a Catholic. But before I lift up the Catholic religion, I'm going to uplift the banner that Jesus died on the cross for me. You look like one of those guys who is sawdust and spit-out nails. I've been where you're at. It doesn't take a man to handle the garbage of the world. I know what it's like. So what is it that I offend you with?"

"I love the Pope! He's second-in-command to God."

"Then tell this donkey-flunked-kindergarten-who-they-threw-out-of-recess, why the Pope drives in a bulletproof car?" I asked. "Did Jesus come on a bulletproof donkey? No, he came here, and he walked and lived among us. So whether you like it or not, I'm going to preach. If you don't like it, just go to your room. I'm going to do what I came to do."

After that, the guy sat down, and he listened.

After the service, everyone left, and the man who had come with me said, "Pablo, I'm not going back into the Details with you because they're going to kill us in there the way you talk to them."

"What are you afraid of?" I asked him.

"Did you see that guy?" he said. "He had a big old scar over here, and no teeth over there. He even had muscles on his lips."

"Bring me the guy who put him in that condition," I said. "And I won't talk to him that way. But this guy, he's lost every battle, man. Don't you see that? He's got a big body, but he's lost every battle."

Another time, after one of my services, a big *grandote* vato stood up and gave a testimony that he didn't believe in none of that stuff I was teaching. He was from Samoa, an island in the South Pacific, and he was doing time.

I let him speak his mind, but later, when I went back to the prison, I went to visit him. I kept visiting him, and even though he didn't like what I was teaching, we became friends. Later, he accepted the Lord.

After he became a Christian, he started writing letters to his wife and thinking about his future. He told me, "Ten years they gave me. I'm going to follow the Lord until I get out, and when I get out, I'll do whatever he asks of me."

After he got out, he wrote me a few letters, and he called me. He told me he got his family back, and he started a business. He's living in Hawaii. He's not on drugs anymore. He told me, "I've got something in my heart now that *rucas* (women) or *feria* can't put there."

CHAPTER 45

Three Crosses

My friend Eddie started going into the prisons with me. When Eddie and I arrived at the prison, guys would look through the bars outside, and they would call out to us. Everybody wanted to come to the service. Nobody forced them.

We would even get the guys who were paralyzed from drugs. They were coming in wheelchairs with bags. They were all gang members I used to know, but they never gave up the crazy life. And they all wound up in prison, doing time. Most of these guys have kidney problems, sclerosis. They're in dialysis.

I tell people, "Nobody cares if you're a paralytic. They'll still send you to prison anyway."

One time we went to the prison in Santa Fe. We were preaching and talking downstairs where they got the hard-cores, and they had a guard stationed there with us.

I told these guys, "When Jesus was crucified, there were three crosses. Jesus was in the middle, and two guys hung on crosses next to him. One on his right and one on his left. They were being executed, too.

"The first guy told Jesus, 'If you're the one you claim to be, then help yourself and help us.'

"But the second guy rebuked the first guy and said, 'We're under the same sentence, and that's the way it should be, because we deserve it. But this man has done nothing.'

"Now, if I go and pull a job, and I get caught pulling a job, then I'm guilty. Why do I need a lawyer when I know I'm guilty? That's how this guy was. He knew he was guilty. So then he turned to Jesus and said, 'Remember me when you reach your kingdom, man.'

"This guy, being an idiot like me, probably never went to the temple, he probably didn't light no candles. He was just a thief, a criminal. He didn't tell Jesus, 'Forgive me. Can I light some candles for you? Can I honor you?' No, all he told him was, 'Remember me when you reach your kingdom.'

"And Jesus looked down at this guy's life, a no-life, and said, 'You'll be with me in paradise.'

"Jesus told him that because everybody deserves a chance. As a matter of fact, this guy went with Jesus before everybody else, and he never did nothing for God."

Eddie and I finished the service, and we left the prison.

Before heading home to Albuquerque, we stopped at the 7-11. I was picking out a sandwich, and a man came up to me. He was a guard from the prison.

"I've been hearing what you guys have been saying when you come to visit," he said, "And you know what? I want to follow the Lord. My family, too."

The guard caught the idea, and he gave his life to the Lord.

CHAPTER 46

A Thousand Hills

I came home from work one day, and Lugie told me, "There's this guy who called you, and he wants you to call him. He's a pastor."

When we were with Barrios, a lady used to come to our church. Her family was dysfunctional, like all of ours. She used to pray with us, and then she got her husband on board. After he worshipped with us for a while, he became a pastor and opened up his own place.

I called the pastor, and he said he used to see me at the restaurant with my Bible. "How would you like to come and help me in the church?" he asked. "You can take over the Wednesday night preaching."

I told him I would do it, but I was going to bring Eddie.

So I started preaching on Wednesday nights. Eddie and I continued to do prison ministry, but we did it under the name of our new pastor's church.

A lot of people were showing up to the services we held on Wednesday nights at the church, and things were going well, but something was bothering Eddie.

Eddie called a meeting with the pastor, and he asked him, "Our church says 'Ministries' in the name, but why don't we have no ministries? We don't feed the hungry here at the church. We don't go out into the streets. We just go over there and get the donuts from Rainbow to feed to the congregation."

Eddie wanted to get the church into street ministry. He wanted us to minister to the drug addicts. And that meant we had to go to where they were. We had to intermingle with them. Their problems had to become our problems.

After the meeting, the pastor told me that Eddie wasn't welcome at the church anymore and that he couldn't go to the prison with me anymore.

"Well, Eddie was going to the prison with me before you," I said. "And I'm not going to drop him just because he's asking you, 'What ministry do you have?'"

But our pastor didn't back down, so I left his church.

Once again, I was without a church.

But I still wanted to preach.

After thinking about it, I decided to start my own service in the back of my house. That Wednesday, instead of going to my former pastor's church, I got together thirty folding chairs and a pulpit, and I set them out in my backyard.

After I set out the chairs in the morning, I went to the restaurant where I study, and I sat at the table with my Bible open. I was so down that day because of what had happened.

I said to God, "I don't have no money. I don't even know what I'm doing, but if you're going to use me and open up something, you're going to have to support it. You tell me in your Word that you own a thousand cattle and a thousand hills. That means you've got money, and I don't."

The manager of the restaurant and I are friends, so after I finished praying, he came over and sat down with me. While we were talking, a bald-headed man walked over. He didn't say anything. He just put a check on my Bible and walked away.

I picked up the check and looked at it. I wasn't good at reading numbers, but I could read one and zero. "One hundred dollars!" I said. Then I put it in my pocket.

I went home, and before the service, I handed Lugie the check and said, "Hey, this guy blessed us with a hundred dollars, man!" Then, I headed out to the backyard.

As I was walking out the door, Lugie called out, "It's not a hundred dollars, Pablo. It's a thousand dollars!"

After that, I never asked the Lord for money again.

People showed up to the service that night in my backyard. Some people were from the Wednesday night service at my former church, even though I had never announced it.

Later that week, Eddie and I went to give a service in the prison like we always did. But this time the lady at the entrance stopped me. "There was a pastor that called," she said. "He said that you guys aren't allowed in the prison anymore. That you were disobedient." I go way back with this girl, so she knew me. "But I didn't believe that," she said. "I didn't pay any attention to that." And she let us in.

When I got home, I called the pastor, and I said, "Hey Pastor, how are you doing?"

"You prostrated my church," he said.

"What do you mean *prostrated*?" I asked.

"You took all my people."

"I didn't even announce that I was leaving your church," I told him. "But, if I had announced it, you would have lost more than a few people. You would have been empty."

Then I said, "I wanted to ask you, how come you called to the prison to give us a bad report? Are you man enough to tell the mothers and fathers that you tried to stop God's Word from being taught to their sons and daughters in prison?"

He got pissed and hung up the phone on me, and it took a long time before we talked again.

CHAPTER 47

His Place

A lot of people started coming to my services, because we didn't preach like other people preached. We preached down and out to the drug addicts. We intermingled with their problems. So they started showing up. I told them about my life and how I had changed, and I taught them how to have a relationship with the Lord, how to live by his Word.

"The man who lives by the sword dies by the sword," I told them. "The sword is whatever drug you're in. If you smoke, you're going to get cancer. If you drink, you're going to get sclerosis. You're going to die of some kind of drug because that's the sword you live by, and that's the sword you'll die by.

"Jesus told Peter, 'Sell everything you've got and buy a sword.' But it wasn't the sword you cut people with. It was the Word.

He told him to sell everything because the sword costs. The Word costs. And you've got to buy it with your obedience."

At my altar call, I had the person read a Prayer of Salvation where they invite the Lord into their life.

> *Lord Jesus, by faith I turn to you now. I ask you to give me the joy and peace of knowing you. I want you to come into my life and be my Lord and Savior. I would ask you to deliver me from the things of this world that stand between you and me. I need you, Lord Jesus. Fill me with your Holy Spirit that I may live free of the attacks of Satan, and free of sickness. Come Lord Jesus, be my Lord and Savior. Amen.*

Sometimes I have to tell a guy, "If you want your wife back, and you said that prayer to the Lord because she's here, but you didn't mean it, *he* did. Once you recite that, even if you didn't mean it, *he* did. He'll hunt you down, man. You'll never get away from him because you already let him in.

"So don't play the part that you're doing this just to get right with your wife and your kids and then continue doing your own garbage. Because even if you didn't mean it, he does. And that's what's important. *¿Que no?*"

After a while, I realized I needed a bigger place for the services. I knew a lady who had a big house, and she rented it to me. We held services there, but after a while, the neighbors started complaining because there were too many cars coming in. I found another place on Coors, but then that place got too small. Finally, I found a larger building for rent on Central. It used to be a gay bar, and the owner decided to rent it to me.

We named our church "His Place."

I told my congregation, "Jesus told a story about a man traveling from Jerusalem to Jericho. The man got beat up and stripped of everything he had. They left him naked, bloody, lying for dead, there on the road.

"A priest came by and looked at him, but he didn't help him. A Levite also passed by him, but when he saw him, he crossed the street. As did the Pharisees and the Sadducees.

"Well, what was this man doing in Jericho? Apparently, he was a worshipper because he was coming from Jerusalem, and that's where they used to go worship. And he was going to Jericho, because Jericho was lot cheaper for them then living in Jerusalem.

"It was like us living in Martineztown. People get a house in the barrio a lot cheaper than the rich people living up in the Heights. This guy was living in Jericho because it was cheaper for him, but it was also dangerous.

"And why did the priest and the Pharisee see him but not help him? Because nothing unclean ever touched the Pharisee. They were so clean, they didn't even help nobody. They were squeaky clean.

"But then there was the Samaritan. Probably, the man lying in the road hated the Samaritan. Because Jews and Samaritans hated each other. But the Samaritan is the one that took him and fed him."

That's why, when somebody comes into our church, whether they're a prostitute or gang member, I still greet them. I still pray for them. I still hug them. They're just as valuable as the one who's clean with a three-piece suit. And a lot of churches ain't like that, I'm sorry to say.

One day, when I went to prison to minister, a clean-cut guy from Mississippi, named Martin, came up to me. He had been a motorcycle member, and he said that nobody from the churches in there ever invited him to go to church when he got out. And I did. I told him, "Whenever you get out, man, just come and see me."

When he got out, I made a place for him to stay in the church. I got him a job at the pancake house. I never asked him how much money he was making at his job. I never asked him if he was tithing to us. That's his beef.

I also took in gang members who had just gotten out of prison. I got these guys under my wing and brought them into my church. They stayed here at the church day and night. We did Bible studies, and I helped them find work. I used to take some of them to work and then pick them up and bring them back.

I never asked them for money. I never asked them to tithe. I never asked them for nothing. I just helped them. They stayed here, and I took care of them.

CHAPTER 48

Juan Baca

One of the most notorious gang members who came to my church was Juan Baca. While he was still in prison, Juan had become a Christian. Juan knew my former pastor, Dan Sanchez, and when Juan got out of prison, Dan got Juan into the men's home. It was the same men's home that we had started with Barrios for Jesus, but it was now part of Victory Outreach.

Juan ended up leaving Victory Outreach because he didn't believe in the system that Victory Outreach had. He saw what I saw. With Victory Outreach, the guys were washing cars and making money, but at the end of the day, all they got was a hamburger and a coke. All of the money they made washing cars went to the church.

One day during a service at His Place, Juan brought a guy with him from his gang who had just gotten out of prison. This guy's name was Sosta. He was a real tall guy, and he was sitting there in a fold-out chair next to Juan, slouched down with his hat on.

In the middle of the service, Jerry, another former inmate, got up to give a testimony. When Jerry started talking at the podium, Sosta jumped out of his chair and pointed his finger at Jerry.

Then he yelled out real loud for everyone to hear, "*Yo tengo papeles en ese vato! Ese vato es r-r-rata!* I've got papers on this vato. He's a rat!"

"Quiet! Sit down!" Juan told him. "You're a new creature now! You're supposed to forgive all that."

Whatever Juan said went, so Sosta sat down, and he stayed quiet.

Juan applied for a job with the city. I gave him my recommendation, and they gave him a temporary job in my department. I became his supervisor. Juan used to drive for me, and I would send him out to do yard work. He was one of the hardest workers in the department. Juan treated everybody just like they did in the 1950s. He showed a lot of *respeto* (respect) to everybody.

Juan used to go with me into the prisons and minister to the vatos. I remember one time we were going to the jail that was near the dump—the place where they throw the garage and the rotten leaves. It stunk like heck. I remember coming out, and there was a girl standing there, waiting for us.

"You killed my brother!" she said to Juan. Her brother had gotten killed in prison by Juan's gang. We just stood there while she told Juan off. Juan didn't have nothing to say. He just felt sorry.

Juan didn't do anything with his gang no more. He got married to a woman named Becky, and they bought a house. He started holding Bible studies in his home. We used to go to his Bible studies.

When Juan became a Christian, a lot of people came to visit him. Notorious vatos, killers from Chicago would come to visit Juan. And he wasn't talking with them about *rollas, cargo, chiva*. He was talking about the Lord. All the time. You couldn't sit with Juan without hearing about the Lord.

I remember meeting a guy from Chicago who had come to visit Juan. He had been a member of the black gangs. He had been in prison with Juan. But he respected Juan enough to come and meet him after he had changed. He gave Juan a couple of suits. This guy also became a pastor.

Juan spent the rest of his years doing Bible studies, going back into jails, talking to people. He died at his house.

CHAPTER 49

A Personal Question

One afternoon, not long before my conversion, I was sitting in my truck in a parking lot, and a panhandler came up to my window. I rolled down my window, and the guy looked at me and said, "Hey, Pablo! Remember me?"

I looked at him a little closer, trying to figure out who he was.

"It's me, Pidox," he said.

"Pidox! It's been a long time!"

I hadn't seen Pidox since we had sat in jail together after being picked up for the sawed-off shotgun. It had been at least twenty years. Pidox was drinking and living on the streets. I hardly recognized him.

He and I talked for a little while. Before he left, I gave him all the change I had in my pocket.

Several years later, I ran into my old friend, Ray. He had opened his own business. He told me that his brother Poncho, who had served time with me in Reno, was dead. When Poncho got out of prison, he had gotten married, but he couldn't find work. One night, he was pulling a job some place and the police shot him in the head and killed him.

Most of my homies from Springer, from la pinta, from the streets were dead. I don't know how it is that I didn't die, too.

I was standing by the door of my church one evening, thinking about all these people I knew from the past, when I saw a car drive through the parking lot. I recognized the driver. He was a guy who used to come to my meetings in prison. So I walked over to his car. "Hey, man! When did you get out? I haven't seen you!"

"Yeah, I just got out," he told me.

"Come on in! We're going to have a Bible study."

"No," he said. "I know God, man. I don't need to go in there. I know God."

That's when I saw the teenage girl sitting in the car next to him.

"Who's this?" I asked.

"This is my daughter."

"Can I ask you a personal question?" I asked her.

"Yes," she said.

"Is this your dad?"

"Yeah, this is my dad."

"Do you know him?" I asked.

She hesitated and then said, "No. I know *of* him."

Because he never was with her. He had done a lot of time.

Then I said to her dad, "That's the way you know God. Like your daughter knows you. You don't know him. You know *of* him."

The guy I was talking to ended up dying of an overdose.

When he went, his family invited me to say words at his eulogy. Lugie went with me, and before the service, we pulled into a parking space at the church.

While I was still buckled in the driver's seat, a guy off of Central came up to my car window. I noticed a big rock in his hand, but before I could do anything, he hit my window with his rock.

The window held, giving me time to unbuckle myself, but then he hit it again, shattering out the glass. The glass cut my face, and blood splattered all over my shirt and pants.

Lugie grabbed my arm and pulled me towards her, yelling for help. The guy tried to reach through the window to hit me in the head with his rock, but I grabbed his hands and thrust him backwards.

Just then, I saw a friend of mine, Frank, came out of the church.

"Get this guy off of me!" I yelled to Frank. "Hold him!"

Frank ran over and grabbed the guy. I jumped out of the car, and Frank and I wrestled the guy down. We didn't beat him up or nothing. We just threw away his rock and calmed him down. I didn't even press charges on him. The police already knew about him.

After that, Lugie and I went into the church, and I did the eulogy all bloodied up.

A few days later, I was studying this passage in the Bible:

"A man said to Jesus, 'Let me first go and bury my father, and then I'll come follow you.' Jesus told him, 'Let the dead bury the dead.'"

"How is that?" I asked God. "How can the dead bury the dead?"

He told me, "When you and him are junkies, and he dies before you, and you go to his funeral, you're just as dead. You just haven't laid down yet. That's the only difference. When you're a junkie, you're just as dead as that guy you're burying. It's just a matter of time and another dead person will bury you."

CHAPTER 50

A Little Badge

I was burying a lot of people. People who were overdosing. So I started a Twelve-Step program with Alcoholics Anonymous (AA) at the church.

We have Twelve Step on Thursday nights at 5:30 at His Place. We have a big meal for everybody — hominy with chicken, beans and chile, tortillas, cookies and cakes, water and cokes. We put the tables back there, and they come from all walks of life. Prostitutes, homeless, addicts — they all come. And we share the Word with them. We do the Recovery Bible.

We get a subject, like on forgiveness. Then we write five names, and we put them in the basket. Whoever picks it gets up to talk about his experience of forgiveness. You can't say that nobody has done you wrong, because we've all been wronged by somebody. The Bible says you can't enter the kingdom unless you forgive.

When you have the love of God in you, you see creation in a different way. In Springer, in jail, in prison, everything is segregated. And the world is like that. Whatever your race is — Spanish, Indian, Black, Anglo — there are certain places you can't go. But the Lord changed me in that way. I traded the wrong for the right. Now I love everybody. Everybody is welcome in my church. Even if they stink.

I wear a patch on my shirt. It's got twelve candles on it, one for each of the twelve steps in AA. I had it on one time when I went to minister in prison. I was holding a service when this guy from the gangs walked in.

I knew he was a gang member because he walked in like he owned the place, like somebody owed him something. His shoe was held together by a Band-Aid. I knew his walk because I had walked that walk.

He walked into the service, and when he saw my Twelve Step badge, he looked at me and said, "Are you the marshal here?"

"Yeah, and you better behave," I said. "We're having a meeting."

So he sat down.

I looked at all the guys sitting there, and I told them, "You know, when you're in prison, there's a guard here that's about ninety-eight years old, and he can't barely walk, and he's a three-time tapper into the system. He's old and he can't fight.

"You're a gorilla out there trying to kill people, but you don't do nothing in front of this old man. He tells you when to go to bed, when to eat. He runs your life. How come? Because he's got that badge.

"That little badge he wears makes all the difference. You don't respect the man. He's so old you could slap him around, and he wouldn't even know where you slapped, but that badge stops you. You know the badge can send you to the hole and make a drop on you, man. So you don't go beyond that badge.

"You let that little badge control you while you're in prison, yet why can't you do the same thing for yourself when you get out? It's because you got out of your little cell, but you didn't get out of prison. You just moved to a bigger prison without bars, which is the world. But you're still the same.

"When you're locked up, you don't take no drugs or nothing. So why don't you try it when you get out? It's the same thing. No pain, no gain. It's what you put into it. That's how come I'm driving a nice car. That's how come I have a nice house. I'm straight. You can do that, too.

"You don't have to go to a program in Chicago to change, because wherever you go, there you are. It's you. You didn't change. If you were a junkie here, you're going to be a junkie over there. Because you don't see it. You're blind. You're behind the veil.

"I've been your age, Bro," I said to the guy who had pointed at my AA badge. "You've never been mine. I've been where you're at. I know how to use the bucket. I know who took your ruca. I know everything. But I want to tell you how I think. God changed me, and you've got a shot at the title too, if you want it. It takes a lot of effort and a lot of work, but you've got it down pat already, Bro.

"Ask yourself right now what you want. Do you always want to be crying to somebody? Do you always want someone to be telling you what to do? Why do you let the devil kick your yo-yo around, man? Why don't you stand up for your rights and claim your life?"

CHAPTER 51

In His Image

One day, I was sitting in the restaurant studying about when Moses led God's people into the desert. It was God's intention to lead them through the desert and into the Promised Land. Do you know how far they were from the Promised Land? Eleven miles. But it took them forty years to get there. For forty years they went around and around in circles.

"I can't understand that," I said to God. "I ran from the police from Alameda to here, which is a little more than eleven miles, in less than half an hour. And these guys took more than forty years to go eleven miles. Why is it that it took them so long to go such a short distance?"

"What are you talking to me for about taking eleven miles?" he said. "It took you thirty years to go eighteen inches."

I tell my congregation, "All this *viaje*—the darkness, the drugs, the prostitution. That's our wilderness experience. It took me thirty years to move eighteen inches in my life. But some of us never even travel those eighteen inches. We're sixty-five, seventy-five, ninety-eight, and we never went even eighteen inches."

I've sent a lot of guys to men's homes. I've married a lot of them that got out of prison, too. Lots of them have come to my church when they got out of prison. I've gotten many letters from guys who have written me over the years.

Different guys from different prisons have told me, "I loved your service. Can you send me here? Can you send me there?"

I would always tell them, "Come on down, man. I'll help you out."

A guy called me not too long ago and told me, "Twenty years ago you talked to me about God in prison. Now, I have my own church, and I'm doing good."

God had done a miracle in my life. I've been at His Place for twenty years now, and we've never been late on the rent once.

My brother Flo is our head usher, and my brother Richard is also a pastor. Eddie passed away and went to be with the Lord.

I've still got some areas to work on. But I'm better today than I was yesterday. I tell people, if you blow yesterday, you can't bring it back. When the Lord picked me up, I wasn't in the garbage can. I was under it. There was no room in the garbage can for me no more.

But today I'm able to talk to people that other people can't talk to because of where I've been. God sees potential in everybody, even someone like me, and that's how I try to see people because we are all created in his image.

I tell people that Jesus said the kingdom of God is within you. If you close your eyes for a moment, you see nothing but darkness. But Jesus says when the light comes in, the darkness leaves.

Yesterday is gone, and tomorrow is unknown. Those things are in darkness. Why don't you live in between the history and the mystery? Live in the light. Live today.